10 FOR 10

10 FOR 10

Hedley Verity and the
Story of Cricket's Greatest Bowling Feat

Chris Waters

B L O O M S B U R Y
LONDON • NEW DELHI • NEW YORK • SYDNEY

Published in the UK by
John Wisden & Co.
An imprint of Bloomsbury Publishing Plc
50 Bedford Square, London WC1B 3DP

www.wisden.com
www.bloomsbury.com

Bloomsbury is a trademark of Bloomsbury Publishing Plc

Bloomsbury Publishing, London, New Delhi, New York and Sydney

A CIP catalogue record for this book is available from the British Library

ISBN 978 1 4729 0890 2

10 9 8 7 6 5 4 3 2 1

Typeset by Saxon Graphics Ltd, Derby
Printed and bound in Great Britain by CPI Group (UK) Ltd, Croydon CR0 4YY

MIX
Paper from
responsible sources
FSC® C020471

In memory of Douglas Verity

Contents

Contents

Verily, virile, Verity
With wonderful skill and dexterity
In a very few overs
He made Notts the rovers
A record to hand to posterity

A verse by a Mr J. B. Frecknall, of Carrington, published in the *Nottingham Evening News* on Saturday 16 July 1932, four days after Hedley Verity's record feat.

I

Starting with Shipston

Cricketers rarely deal in statistical perfection. Don Bradman's Test average was 99.94, agonisingly short of the magical figure; Jim Laker took all but one of Australia's 20 wickets during the Old Trafford Test of 1956, while Hanif Mohammad ran himself out on 499, for Karachi against Bahawalpur in 1959. If Bradman had managed just four more runs, Laker obtained just one more wicket, and Hanif successfully made good his ground, all would have brought off the beau ideal. As it was, they created new standards of excellence, inviting their fellows to go a step further. In 1932, however, came a feat so flawless, so symmetrically stunning, it was the nonpareil of numerical Utopia. Hedley Verity's 10 for 10, for Yorkshire versus Nottinghamshire at Leeds, has an air of amazement that glows to this day. "Had it been 10 for 12, 10 for 11 or 10 for 9, it wouldn't have had the same striking impact," said Douglas Verity, a suitably proud son. "There's something about it that sounds so special; it just has a wonderfully musical ring." Verity's return – sealed with seven wickets in 15 balls, including the hat-trick – is the greatest recorded in first-class cricket. His full figures were 19.4 overs, 16 maidens, 10 runs, 10 wickets.

Even more incredible, Verity's feat was immediately followed by an unbroken stand of 139 between the Yorkshire opening batsmen Percy Holmes and Herbert Sutcliffe that took their team to a 10-wicket victory. On the same pitch on which Verity caused chaos, Holmes and Sutcliffe repelled an attack that included pace bowlers Harold Larwood and Bill Voce, who'd gain notoriety that winter in the Bodyline series. Although Verity was helped by a drying surface after torrential rain, the consensus was that only part-explained his tour de force. According to newspaper reports, there was no rational reason for the disparity between his performance and that of Holmes and Sutcliffe. "The wicket was never the vexatious proposition the Notts' batsmen made it out to be," observed the *Nottingham Evening News*, while the *Yorkshire Post* declared that the pitch "could not have changed so completely as the difference in the two innings would suggest". The *Nottingham Journal* said: "The feat was sensational."

My own fascination with Verity's feat began when I chanced to meet one of his victims. In December 2000, my then employer, the *Nottingham Evening Post*, sent me to interview Frank Shipston, a former Nottinghamshire batsman who'd become the oldest living county cricketer, aged 94, after the death of 103-year-old ex-Derbyshire batsman Jimmy Hutchinson. Although Shipston was a modest player who scored 1,183 runs in 49 first-class games at 18.48, I discovered while making some preliminary research that he'd actually played in this phenomenal match. In fact, he was its last survivor and had been Verity's second victim, joint top-scoring with 21 along with fellow opener Walter Keeton.

When I visited Shipston at his home in Nottingham, the first words of a robust nonagenarian to the shy 20-some-thing standing on his doorstep were full of smiling irony. "Oh, you're a young chap," he chuckled. Shipston, a widower who lived with his son, Peter, and family, offered a warm handshake and led the way into a living room that contained no sign of his former occupation. Then, after modestly stating that "I can't understand why anyone should want to interview a nothing cricketer like me", Shipston – six-foot tall and strong-built – cast his mind back 75 summers to the days of Jack Hobbs and Wally Hammond, tram cars and steam trains, cat's whisker radios and silent pictures.

"I'll never forget my first day at Trent Bridge," he announced, a faraway look in his kindly eyes. "It was 1925 and I'd gone for a trial after being spotted playing for my colliery team. I was putting on my pads when Jimmy Iremonger, the Notts' coach, pulled me to one side. 'See that lad?' he said, pointing to one of the bowlers in the distance. 'He's a little bit quick, so watch the ball closely.' I said, 'Thanks very much' and got ready to take guard, although I took his words with a pinch of salt. Well, the first ball from this chap called Harold Larwood whizzed past at the speed of light and hit the net before I'd seen it. The second hit me flush in the goolies and left me doubled-up in agony. One of the senior pros pointed out that I wasn't wearing a box. So there I was, batting against Larwood, and I wasn't even wearing a box; to be honest, I was so wet behind the ears I didn't know what a box was."

Despite his painful introduction, Shipston was awarded a three-year contract. He made his debut in the final match of the 1925 season, against Glamorgan at Swansea, exchanging life in the pits for life in the fresh air. "Suddenly, I went from working in the pitch-black to enjoying lovely summer's days all around the country," he recalled. "I couldn't believe how lucky I was."

Although my newspaper only wanted an overview of Shipston's career, I was primarily interested in the 10 for 10.

Mere mention of it drew an embarrassed laugh and a roll of
the eyes, as though he'd remembered some childhood caper.
"My word, the great Hedley Verity," sighed Shipston. "What
a name to conjure with." My companion's voice trailed away
and a sorrowful expression came over his face. He turned his
head to look out of the window, staring sadly at the wintry
scene. "Killed in the war, of course," he whispered. "Such a
fine chap, and such a fine bowler."

The feat took place on the third and last day when the game
appeared to be drifting to a draw. Nottinghamshire had
scored 234 in their first innings, Yorkshire replying with 163
for nine before declaring at the start of the day to try to make
a game of it. Shipston and Keeton made comfortable progress
as Nottinghamshire sought to bat out time. They took the
score to 44 for nought before the visitors collapsed to 67 all
out, Holmes and Sutcliffe speeding Yorkshire home with
their century partnership. Shipston corroborated newspaper
reports that conditions were not over-biased towards Verity.
"I remember there'd been a storm the night before and play
began late on the final day, but you couldn't attribute
Hedley's success to the state of the wicket. It offered him a
certain amount of assistance, and he was able to get the ball
to lift when the sun came out and dried the pitch, but Holmes
and Sutcliffe put the conditions into proper context. As I
recall, Hedley wasn't spinning it much – just enough to find
the edge. But that's all a spinner has to do."

Shipston's memories – sepia-coated and clouded by time –
returned in dribs and drabs, like water dripping from a temper-
amental tap. He couldn't remember specific match detail and
occasionally got frustrated. "I'm afraid I don't recall any of the
wickets or anything, and I can't remember how I was out. Still,

it was 70-odd years ago. These days, I have trouble remembering what I did yesterday." However, Shipston did his best to satisfy my interest – even though it seemed almost painful to think back so far. "It's funny, but the thing that sticks in my mind is that I ended up with the captain's batting gloves. Arthur Carr was the Notts' captain and quite a character. He used to frighten me because you never knew what he'd do next. I remember a game at Cardiff. After the lads had been drinking at night, Carr walked on to the pitch, whipped out his middle stump and watered the wicket, encouraging the rest of us to follow suit. He reckoned the pitch had been favouring the batsmen. Anyway, when Verity got him that day at Leeds, Carr stormed back to the dressing room and threw his green batting gloves on to the floor. The gloves happened to land at my feet. 'You can ruddy well have 'em,' he said."

Shipston's only other recollection was of the eerie silence among his team-mates after the match. Even the garrulous Carr was speechless as Verity's performance slowly sank in. "That silence was like nothing I experienced in cricket. We just sat in the pavilion, staring into space. We couldn't comprehend what had happened. One minute, the game was a draw. The next, we'd lost it in a jiffy. None of us knew what the hell to say. And all the while the Yorkshire crowd were cheering and chanting wildly outside. Chanting the name of the great Hedley Verity."

Shipston left Trent Bridge the following year to join Nottingham City Police Force. He served for 14 years as a constable and then took a job with a laundry firm. In 1956, Shipston returned to the first-class game. He had one season on the umpires' list, standing in 22 Championship fixtures. The following year, Shipston returned to Nottinghamshire as coach – a position he held until 1966.

"We were rubbish, though, no better than a Minor Counties side. We had one good player in Reg Simpson, and that was about it." After leaving Trent Bridge for the last time, Shipston became a newsagent.

When we met on that day of warm reminiscence, Shipston told me his only significant impairment was deteriorating eyesight, which meant he read with a magnifying glass. He was proud of the fact that he walked every day for 45 minutes and attributed his age to a life of moderation and good genes. "I think the Shipstons must be made of solid material," he said. "My father had rheumatic fever twice and, when he contracted it many years ago, once was a killer, but father lasted into his 80s." Shipston junior lasted to within touching distance of three figures. He was just over three weeks short of his 99th birthday when he died on 6 July 2005, having been not only the oldest county cricketer but the world's oldest first-class cricketer – a mantle that befell him on 9 June 2004 following the death of 101-year-old former Western Australia leg-spinner Ted Martin. Shipston retained an avid interest in cricket right until his death. Peter Wynne-Thomas, the Nottinghamshire County Cricket Club librarian, recalled that Shipston rang him five days earlier. "One of Frank's questions centred on Stephen Fleming, the captain Notts had signed from New Zealand for the 2005 season. There was none of the usual retired cricketer's claptrap on how much better the players were in his day. Frank was still interested in cricket and Notts cricket especially. He appreciated the game and what it had done for him."

It was an appreciation I'd experienced when I'd interviewed Shipston, and although he'd spoken of his embarrassment at having been on the wrong end of Verity's feat, I

Shipston family collection

The last survivor of the 10 for 10 match: Frank Shipston on the day he was interviewed by the author.

sensed that, deep down, he was proud of his part in it, proud of having shared the stage with such as Holmes and Sutcliffe, Larwood and Voce. I can still hear his parting words as he bade me farewell. "Years ago, you could leave your front door unlocked and go out for the day; nowadays, you have to lock it even if you're inside the house. Oh well, thanks for coming, and sorry I wouldn't have been much help."

Six weeks before Shipston passed away, I'd been brought into even closer contact with the 10 for 10. In May 2005, having by then left the *Nottingham Evening Post* to become cricket correspondent of the *Yorkshire Post*, I found myself holding the very ball with which Verity performed his miracle feat. It happened when Yorkshire County Cricket Club held an exhibition to mark the centenary of the left-arm spinner's birth. As part of the celebrations, Verity's son, Douglas, brought several items of memorabilia from his home in North Wales, including the 10 for 10 ball. The exhibition coincided with Yorkshire's County Championship match against Essex, which was renamed The Hedley Verity/ Green Howards Memorial Match after the club obtained permission from the England and Wales Cricket Board. Verity was a captain in the Yorkshire-based army regiment when he died of injuries during the Allied invasion of Sicily in 1943. He was 38. The memorabilia was displayed behind lock and key in the Headingley Long Room and attracted significant interest from spectators.

I attended the exhibition and introduced myself to Douglas. I told him of my admiration for his father's feat and the precious afternoon I'd spent with Frank Shipston. Later that day, a tall, distinguished gentleman with silver hair and a ready smile suddenly appeared at my side in the press box. It was Douglas Verity. "Here you go, lad," he said, pushing a cricket ball into my hand. "You told me you were interested in Dad's 10 for 10; well, I thought I'd bring the ball over from the Long Room so you could have a proper look at it, away from the crowds." The ball was dark-red and what particularly struck me was its size; it seemed slightly smaller than modern balls, although the law in 1932 allowed for the same variation in weight and circumference as today. A silver seam was wrapped around the ball and inscribed:

Y.C.C.C.
PRESENTED TO H. VERITY
TO COMMEMORATE
10 WICKETS FOR 10 RUNS v NOTTS.
JULY 12th 1932.

As I chatted with Douglas, several journalists gathered round. Suddenly, Yorkshire versus Essex was being played in front of reporters oblivious to the match as the 10 for 10 ball became the centre of attention. Some of my colleagues observed it with reverence, as though in the presence of a holy relic. Others tossed it around in their hands and doubtless let their imaginations wander. A few days later, I wrote a column for the *Yorkshire Post* sharing my experience with readers. I told how Verity's record astonished me and how privileged I'd felt to have held the ball. I added that if I possessed a time machine I could think of no passage of play I would rather watch. The column inspired a letter from a gentleman who wrote on a sheet of bright yellow notepaper headed with the words "I was there!"

> *Dear Mr Waters,*
> *It has been a pleasure to read your article on Hedley*
> *Verity and his marvellous 10 for 10.*
> *That Tuesday morning in 1932 I left Woodhouse Grove*
> *School with two of my friends with their father to go to*
> *Headingley. The game with Notts had already begun;*
> *the score was 20 runs for no wickets.*
> *So we saw all the wickets fall, but I cannot remember how.*
> *It has been one of my life's joys to recount this notable*
> *occasion.*
> *Yours sincerely*
> *John Robert Richardson (90 and a half)*

The letter contained no phone number, only an address. When I telephoned directory enquiries, I discovered the number was ex-directory. With an idea I might one day write in greater detail on the 10 for 10, I drove on spec to the house in Earby, a small town just inside the Lancashire border, which was once part of the West Riding of Yorkshire. A woman answered the door and said that Mr Richardson was her father, who lived with her and her husband. She invited me into a spacious lounge where I found Mr Richardson – dapper in a navy blazer, white shirt and dark tie – sitting on a sofa watching cricket on television. Small in stature and mild of manner, he greeted me with the warmest of smiles. Like Shipston, Mr Richardson was in fine condition for a nonagenarian and, like Shipston, retained priceless memories of the atmosphere and occasion. "I can still picture Verity running into bowl. He was operating from the Rugby Stand end and we were sitting somewhere near the pavilion, which in those days was right next to that end and more or less diagonal to the pitch. I was in my late teens and a boarder at Woodhouse Grove School, just a few miles from the ground at Apperley Bridge. We went to the game in my friend's father's car – a Rover I think it was. Funnily enough, it was the only time I saw Verity play. It was the school holidays and we just picked that day completely out the blue. At the time, I didn't appreciate how unique it was. It was only as the years went by that I appreciated it more. But I've always carried with me that sense of occasion, that sense of the impossible."

Mr Richardson recalled the excitement as the drama unfolded. He said the noise got louder with the fall of each wicket. "The reaction of the crowd has always stayed with me. There could only have been a couple of thousand people in the ground but there was great cheering and clapping, which seemed to get louder with every dismissal, and the wickets went so fast it never seemed to stop. I don't think people could believe what was happening, but there were no wild scenes among Yorkshire's players. The mood on the field was fairly restrained. There was none of the hugging that goes on now. When the last wicket fell, Verity simply shook hands with his team-mates and politely acknowledged the crowd. I remember thinking that he seemed so modest."

After Holmes and Sutcliffe knocked off the runs, Mr Richardson tried to get Verity's autograph. But with so many clamouring for the hero's signature, and with his friend's father needing to get home, it wasn't possible. "Verity was mobbed when he returned to the pavilion. A sea of people seemed to swallow him up. He came out after a while to sign people's scorecards. He was signing them faster than they were shoved in his hand. Unfortunately, I couldn't get near him because the queues were too big, but just to have been there was enough for me."

After exhausting all memory of the momentous day, Mr Richardson asked if I would like to hear him play the piano.

"I was there!" – John Robert Richardson, one of the privileged few who saw Hedley Verity's world record feat.

Rosemary/Stan Norkett

Classical music was another great love and I left him playing
Debussy's *Clair de Lune* in a corner of the lounge, blissfully
wrapped in a world of his own. Mr Richardson, who spent
his working life as a sales representative in the Midlands,
died in 2009, aged 94. There could have been no prouder
witness to sporting history.

Another said to have been at Headingley that day was the
novelist J. L. Carr. Born at Thirsk Junction, North Yorkshire,
in 1912, "Jim" or James Carr was a keen cricket lover and
eccentric character. He was head teacher of a primary school in
Kettering until the age of 55 before leaving to devote himself
fully to writing. In total, Carr wrote/published eight novels, 20
books of wood engravings, 40 county maps and around 80

Bob Carr/The Quince Tree Press

small books. There were a
number of quirky diction-
aries – including, in 1977, his
celebrated *Carr's Dictionary
of Extra-Ordinary Cricketers*.
This comprised 126 entries
ranging from Dr Arthur
Abraham, who "so resembled
his twin, a heavy run-getter,
that opponents frequently
complained to umpires that
he had already batted", to I.
Zingari, "a daring boatman
who promoted cricket
matches on the Goodwin
Sands at low tide" and who
has "no known connection
with a club of that name,

*The novelist J. L. Carr, who
claimed to have left Headingley
prior to the 10 for 10 fearing rain
and condemned himself to "a
lifetime of bitter remorse".*

founded 1846". Under the letter V, which included Captain Vinegar, an 18th-century "owner of a bruisers' agency much employed by cricket game promoters to put down hooligans", was a brief entry for Hedley Verity. Carr claimed to have left Headingley prior to the 10 for 10 fearing rain and condemned himself to "a lifetime of bitter remorse". But although Tuesday 12 July 1932 dawned grey and gloomy, the weather brightened appreciably and Carr's son, Robert, believes that his father – who died in 1994 – might have got his memories muddled. "Was he there? I'm not so sure that he was. Father could be a bit of a romantic. He was a Yorkshireman, of course, and a keen cricket lover, but I never heard him mention the 10 for 10. If he had gone to the game, I'm absolutely certain he would have told me."

Whatever the reality, the fact remains only a privileged few saw Verity spin his way into the record books. Not many could say, à la John Robert Richardson, those magical words, "I was there!"

2

Verity's Rise

At the time of his record performance, Hedley Verity was 27 and in his second full season of first-class cricket. He was a late arrival to the county game having learnt his trade in the Lancashire leagues. Although born close to Headingley stadium, and raised and schooled locally, Verity only prospered in cricket when he moved to the opposite side of the Pennines. He played for Accrington in 1927 and Middleton from 1928 to 1930, the year he made his Yorkshire debut.

It was while at Middleton that Verity made a momentous decision: he changed from bowling seam to spin. Previously he'd been a medium pacer who'd risen no higher than the Yorkshire second team, but the club had several bowlers like that and he was no better than the rest. To achieve his dream of playing professionally, he was advised by the former Yorkshire and England all-rounder George Hirst – who'd recommended he gain experience in Lancashire and continued to coach him back in Yorkshire – that he'd be better changing his modus operandi. Hirst's ex-colleague, Wilfred Rhodes, the Yorkshire and England left-arm spinner who'd reigned supreme since Victorian times, was nearing retirement and the club would need someone to fill his shoes.

Verity adapted so well to Hirst's suggestion he became 10 times the bowler virtually overnight. In 1929, he took 100 wickets for Middleton to top the Central Lancashire League averages and produced a pivotal performance when asked to

Verity with George Hirst, who advised him to take up spin bowling.

stand in for the Yorkshire Seconds against an amateur side. After the Seconds scored 420, the amateurs followed-on 229 runs behind and were routed for 56, Verity taking five for seven. Verity's climb continued when he made his first-class debut in a friendly fixture in May 1930. He returned match figures of three for 96 against Sussex at Huddersfield as the non-playing Rhodes reviewed him through binoculars. A few days later, Verity's first Championship appearance brought match figures of eight for 60 against Leicestershire at Hull, and he ended the season with 64 wickets at 12.42, topping not only the Yorkshire averages but the national ones too. When Rhodes retired that autumn after taking a world record 4,204 wickets at 16.72, to go with 39,969 runs at 30.81, he handed the baton to Verity in a manner befitting his gruff reputation. "He'll do," Rhodes instructed the Yorkshire committee, the cricketing equivalent of a papal decree.

Hedley Verity was born on 18 May 1905 at 4 Welton Grove, Leeds. His father, Hedley Verity senior, was a coal merchant, an occasional lay preacher and chair of the local urban district council. His chief claim to fame – apart from fathering the man who recorded cricket's best bowling figures – was that he drove one of the first tramcars in Leeds. A little under six feet tall, with a sturdy physique, Verity senior had short blond hair parted from left to right, a black moustache, a square jaw, prominent ears, thoughtful eyes and the look of a man who aspired to make a difference in his local community. When Hedley was two, his family moved one-and-a-half miles south to the suburb of Armley, where his father gained work with a coal firm. Two years later, they relocated seven miles north to the village of Rawdon, where his father acquired one

Verity family collection

The young Hedley in his father's coal cart. Verity senior is pictured far right.

of the firm's agencies. Verity senior soon gained sufficient supplies to start his own business, which he ran from the family home – Sefton House. A cosy, stone-built cottage once used to weave wool imported from Australia, it still stands near the junction of the Leeds and Harrogate roads.

Hedley and his father had a close relationship. It was built on a passionate love of cricket and it was said that Hedley could talk to him freely. His mother, Edith, was the steel of the family. Pretty and petite, with a selfless nature, she ensured that her husband's customers never wanted for a cup of tea, a slice of cake or just a chat before paying their coal bills. Verity was blessed with a happy childhood. Sefton House was filled with music and he took part in sing-songs with his parents and siblings – sisters Grace (born 1907) and Edith (born 1916). Grace became a schoolteacher in Rawdon, where her pupils included the Yorkshire cricketers Brian Close and Bryan Stott. She loved to tell how the young Hedley tried to swap her for a neighbour's rabbit, seizing the creature and its hutch and ordering his mother to "give that woman the baby". Hedley instead got a mongrel called Prince, his inseparable boyhood companion.

Prince received a royal view of his master's formative steps in the game. He'd watch for hours as Verity bowled pieces of coal at the shed door and practised batting in his bedroom with predictable consequences for the family furniture. The dog accompanied him to his first proper practices at Rawdon Cricket Club, where Verity would toss his coat on the ground and tell Prince to guard it for all he was worth. After practice, Verity would ask his friends to retrieve the coat – and laugh as Prince refused to give it up as though protecting the last bone in Christendom. Verity played his first competitive cricket at

Yeadon and Guiseley Secondary School and for Rawdon second team. His first match for the Rawdon first team came as a 16-year-old in 1921. It wasn't an auspicious start; Verity was bowled for a golden duck and not brought on to bowl. Better results followed, and he was invited to the Headingley nets after being spotted during a scouting programme run by Hirst and Bobby Peel, the former Yorkshire and England left-arm spinner and Rhodes's predecessor in the county side. Peel, who'd been suspended by the club in 1897 for turning up drunk to a match at Bramall Lane, couldn't understand why the tall, athletic Verity was incapable of generating significant speed. "It's a pity," Peel told him, "you're a good fast bowler wasted."

Undeterred, Verity returned to Rawdon and shone with the bat as much as the ball. A tall and technically correct right-hander, he was thought to be a promising batsman before his bowling came to the fore. In 1924, Verity moved to near neighbours Horsforth Hall Park and, in the last of his three seasons with them, took 62 wickets at an average of nine to win the Yorkshire Council League junior prize. A disappointing summer followed at Accrington, where his first professional engagement was undermined by the condescending attitude of senior players, who didn't enjoy being coached by a novice. Verity started the season encouragingly but his form tailed off like a shooting star. So much so, the club secretary lamented: "Our choice of professional, so very bright at the opening, did not turn out to be quite the success we had thought. It was very discouraging to the players and undoubtedly had an effect on their play." Redemption arrived at Middleton, where Verity got on well with colleagues mostly his own age. After an unremarkable first season, when his output was ordinary, the change to left-arm spin worked wonders and signposted the road into the Yorkshire first team.

Verity family collection

Verity in his days with Yorkshire Colts (Arthur Mitchell is far left of shot).

Verity's apprenticeship – protracted by modern standards – was marked by unusual strength of character. After leaving school at 14, he worked in his father's coal depot, where everything he did was tailored towards the long-term goal of playing for Yorkshire. Even gruelling manual tasks were performed with the master plan firmly in mind. Verity shovelled extra coal just to improve his strength and stamina and delighted in watching his arm muscles grow. Displaying an appetite for fitness ahead of his time, he undertook rigorous skipping in the house and garden and spent his evenings running around the streets of Rawdon, wearing heavy boots to tire himself out. Although supportive of his son's ambitions, Verity senior was anxious he had a career to fall back on. He hired a private tutor with a view to helping him gain secretarial and accountancy qualifications, only to be told: "It's no use, Dad, you're wasting your money. I've made up my mind to someday play for Yorkshire."

Verity senior kept a private memoir of his son's earliest years, which he scribbled on scrap paper in his coal depot. One passage highlights the young man's self-discipline. "Verity's time was so fully occupied in the cricket field that he had no time for anything else," wrote his father. "Any friends he found must, if they wished to retain his friendship, go with him to the cricket field. Some joined the club, but I am afraid most of them found companionship elsewhere. For the same reason he had no girlfriends. He could not afford to waste his time on such business." Throughout his one-man mission to play for Yorkshire, Verity was motivated by a motto that hung on a plaque above his bed. "They told him it couldn't be done, he made up his mind that it could – and he did it."

The side into which Verity brought his 10 for 10 stardust was built along comparable lines. To call it a hard school would be an understatement; the metaphorical cane and slipper were rarely idle in the masters' studies. In this case, the masters were Rhodes and Emmott Robinson, the latter an equally dour all-rounder who'd broken into the first team in 1919, aged 35, and who'd play until he was 47. Robinson, who scored just under 10,000 runs and took just over 900 wickets with his right-arm fast-medium, epitomised the "give-'em-now't" philosophy of Yorkshire cricket. Neville Cardus called him "the personification of Yorkshire cricket" and famously wrote: "I imagine that the Lord one day scooped up a heap of Yorkshire clay, breathed into it and said, 'Emmott Robinson, go on and bowl at the pavilion end for Yorkshire.'" Cardus said Robinson was "as Yorkshire as Ilkley Moor or

Pudsey" and insisted "few have absorbed the game, the Yorkshire game, into their systems, their minds, nerves and bloodstream as Emmott did". Cardus added that the diminutive, bandy-legged Robinson viewed Yorkshire cricket as "a way of living, as important as stocks and shares".

Verity owed much to the guidance of Robinson and, in particular, that of Rhodes, with whom he played five times during Rhodes's last season in 1930. Bill Bowes, the Yorkshire fast bowler who made his first team debut the previous year, and

Ron Deaton collection

Emmott Robinson, whom Neville Cardus called "the personification of Yorkshire cricket".

became one of Verity's closest friends, recalled how the two pros collared them on away trips during that 1930 campaign and dissected their performances with surgical precision. These late-night tutorials, enshrined in folklore, were of a type that could scarcely be imagined today, when any young bowler taking a five-wicket haul is immediately hailed "the next big thing". In his autobiography, Bowes wrote:

> *Every night at about 10.30 those two would come and collect us in the hotel lounge and off we went to a bedroom. There the shaving stick, toothbrush, hairbrush and contents of a dressing-case would be pushed around the eiderdown*

to represent the fieldsmen as all our mistakes of the day
were discussed in detail. They were hard and exacting
taskmasters, but they were right, always right.

Bowes remembered one class particularly after Verity took
seven wickets against Hampshire at Bournemouth. Bowes,
in contrast, had a disappointing day, managing one wicket:

We found Emmott and Wilfred awaiting us in the lounge
when Hedley and I returned from the pictures. "We've
been waiting a long time – we'd better go, else it'll take
till midnight," Wilfred growled. What, I wondered, had I
done wrong? But there was no comment as we filed from
the lounge to the quiet regions upstairs. We entered
Emmott's room and, with a skill born of practice and a
thorough appreciation of the job in hand, the masters
placed their fieldsmen – the customary toilet articles – in
position on the eiderdown. I obviously must be the
culprit. My bowling figures for that day had shown 20
overs, four maidens, 43 runs and only one wicket. Hedley
could rest assured. He was all right – with 24.4 overs, 11
maidens, 26 runs and seven wickets. But as the toilet
articles were placed in position, I saw that they did not
represent the field I had been using. "Now then,
Hedley," said Emmott, "what did you do today?"
Hedley stuck both his hands into his pockets, stuck out his
chest, did a little pleased bend at the knees like a
contented father with his back to the fire talking to his
son, smiled and replied, "Seven for 26, Emmott." Emmott
smote the woodwork at the foot of the bed in disgust.
"Aye, seven for 26, an' it owt to 'a' bin seven for 22! Ah
nivver saw such bowlin'. Whativver wa' t'doin' to gie
AK Judd that fower?"

"How could any young man," Bowes continued, "coming into such an atmosphere, get a swollen head? Yet they were not ogres, and they believed the best time to tell a lad his failings was when he was riding on top of the world, not when he was down."

Popperfoto/Getty Images

Verity savoured such attention to detail. Rhodes and Robinson's adamantine assessments chimed with his thirst for self-improvement. Verity wasted no time implementing his teachers' advice.

Wilfred Rhodes, Verity's mentor and predecessor in the Yorkshire side, who took more than 4,000 wickets and scored just under 40,000 runs.

In 1931, he took 188 wickets at 13.52 to finish second in the national averages to Harold Larwood. He won his first Test cap, against New Zealand at The Oval, collecting four wickets in an innings victory. Verity's performances that summer saw him named one of *Wisden*'s Five Cricketers of the Year along with Bowes, New Zealand batsman Stewie Dempster, Sussex all-rounder Jim Langridge and Oxford University batsman Nawab of Pataudi. But the highlight of his first full season came on 18 May 1931, his 26th birthday, when he achieved something that eluded even Rhodes during a career that spanned a record 1,100 games. He took – for the only other time in first-class cricket – 10 wickets in an innings, returning 10 for 36 against Warwickshire at Headingley.

Verity was only the second Yorkshire player to achieve the feat in first-class matches after Alonzo Drake, a left-arm medium-pacer who'd captured 10 for 35 against Somerset at Weston-super-Mare in 1914. Asked to comment on his efforts by the *Yorkshire Evening News*, Verity – always a reluctant interviewee – said: "Mitchell (Arthur) did some wonderful fielding, and it was one of those rare days when everything is set right for the bowler at one end, but not for the man at the other end." Verity's wife, Kathleen, was more loquacious, telling the reporter she'd missed the morning session due to a headache but that Yorkshire's first home game of the season ultimately proved too great a draw. Mrs Verity said she arrived at the ground shortly after lunch and took her seat inconspicuously in the crowd, adding that it was not long before she was blushing at the favourable comments directed towards her husband. "It is very nice to be a cricketer's wife among a crowd when he is in form, but, then, matters might have been quite the opposite, and the comments would have made me blush just the same," she declared. "Everybody was hoping that 'Mac' [George Macaulay] would not take the last wicket, and that seemed to be the general comment. Perhaps 'Mac' understood. At all events, he did not take a wicket, stout chap! If my headache had not disappeared by that last over, I had forgotten all about it." Macaulay, a fiery off-spinner who played eight Tests, was operating at the other end both times Verity took 10 wickets in an innings for Yorkshire. After Verity's ninth wicket against Nottinghamshire, Macaulay remarked to a team-mate: "If he's good enough to get nine, let him earn the 10th. I shall get it if I can."

Verity's performance against Warwickshire was payback. In 1928, while struggling in his debut season with Middleton, he'd gone for a trial at Edgbaston on the recommendation of Headingley groundsman Ted Leyland, father of Yorkshire

and England batsman Maurice. Verity got no joy against a
Scottish batsman called Henry Roll, who comfortably coun-
tered him on a bone-hard net wicket. It took the Warwickshire
committee all of 10 minutes to decide that Verity wasn't up
to scratch. Warwickshire weren't exactly the shrewdest
judges of talent at the time. They also rejected Bowes before
his Yorkshire debut, while tucked away in the Edgbaston
committee minutes of 4 October 1897 is the immortal line:
"It was decided that, on account of the heavy expenses
already incurred in connection with next year's ground staff,
an engagement could not be offered W. Rhodes of
Huddersfield." Warwickshire thus turned down the man
with the most wickets in the game's history, the man with
the best bowling figures and, in Bowes, a man cricket writer
Raymond Robertson-Glasgow called "the most difficult
fast-medium bowler in England". Between them, Verity,
Rhodes and Bowes took 7,799 first-class wickets.

After his 10-wicket triumph against Warwickshire, Verity
was acclaimed the new Rhodes. The comparison was under-
standable but unsuitable; in bowling method and physical
appearance, the two were as different as the sun and moon.
Rhodes, five feet eight inches, was ruddy-cheeked, flint-eyed
and poker-faced. He wore a flat cap pulled tight over his
forehead and bowled at an orthodox pace for a slow left-
armer. Rhodes tempted batsmen to destruction with a
subtlety that belied his sombre exterior. He was adept at
flighting the ball and as systematically accurate as a Swiss
timepiece. Rhodes's style was as straightforward as the man;
a few short strides to the wicket were followed by a beautifully balanced sideways swing, his right arm high, his left
arm low to the grass before he brought it over smoothly, like
a see-saw moving from bottom to top.

Verity was six foot one inches and solidly built, tipping the scales at 13 stone. He had an angular face, frank and friendly eyes and, according to Robertson-Glasgow, "the look and carriage of a man likely to do supremely well something that would need time and trouble". Verity was prematurely grey in his early 20s and exuded wisdom beyond his years. As reserved and reticent as Rhodes was severe, he took a longer run to the crease than his mentor, gliding towards the stumps as a swan glides elegantly along a stream. He approached softly over seven paces, bowled on his toes and followed through with an expectant flourish; his appeals were often so quiet they could only be heard by the batsman and umpire at the non-striker's end. Whereas Rhodes bowled with his wrist underneath the ball, Verity gripped it tightly across the seam with three fingers so that it barely brushed his palm. He operated at a pace closer to Derek Underwood than that of Monty Panesar and had the ability to make the ball lift. It was Verity's bounce, as much as his spin, that so inconvenienced batsmen. Verity himself said that he and Rhodes had only two things in common: they bowled left-arm spin and liked taking wickets. Rhodes also rubbished attempts to bracket them. In later years, when asked whether there was any ball that Verity bowled that he himself didn't bowl, Rhodes replied, "Aye, there was the ball they cut for four." The implication – beneath the black humour – was that Verity was never a second Rhodes, but always a first Verity.

Wonderful though his form had been in 1931, and despite the flattering if flawed comparison with his predecessor, Verity was by no means certain of retaining his place for England's next major assignment: the 1932–33 tour of Australia. Not only did he face competition from such as

Somerset left-arm spinner Jack "Farmer" White, but the Australian pitches were traditionally unsuited to his style of bowling. Verity went into his record-breaking 1932 season knowing that he would have to produce something truly special to make the trip. Not even in his wildest dreams could he have envisaged how special it would turn out to be.

3

The Background and Build-up

Little Princess Margaret, the daughter of the Duke and Duchess of York, has had a new experience. She has been to her first party, and although she was one of the youngest guests invited, she thoroughly enjoyed herself. Princess Margaret, who will not be two until August, was taken to the party with great dignity by her elder sister, Princess Elizabeth. The children were in charge of their nurse. Princess Margaret entered into the fun as soon as she arrived, and she seemed to enjoy every moment of it. She played and romped with the other children, chatting away to them, obviously delighted with her first venture into social life, and her happy laugh and joyful prattle helped to make the afternoon a great success. Princess Elizabeth enjoyed herself too.

Such was the news in the *Yorkshire Post* on Saturday 9 July 1932, the opening day of the 10 for 10 game. It was a different world, a more innocent world, and newspapers captured that long-lost age. An advertisement in the *Yorkshire Evening News*, promoting a vacuum cleaner, announced: "No husband can invest 10 shillings to better purpose", while another proclaimed: "For your throat's sake, smoke fresh Craven A, made especially to prevent sore throats." Readers were told: "They do not bring about that unpleasant huskiness of the throat so generally peculiar to some cigarettes." There were reports that Chelsea Football Club had spent

£21,000 on wages, benefits and transfers during the 1931–32 season (around £750,000 today), that Laurel and Hardy were on their way to Leeds, and that arrangements were afoot to present the blind composer Frederick Delius with the freedom of his home city of Bradford. Later that month, Jelka Delius would guide her husband's hand over the Certificate of Acceptance at their home in Grez-sur-Loing, northern France.

The leading news story came from the shores of Lake Geneva, where delegates at the Lausanne Conference in Switzerland had voted to suspend First World War reparations payments imposed on defeated countries by the Treaty of Versailles. The treaty compelled Germany to accept full responsibility for causing the war and to pay Allied nations around £6.6 billion, but with the world in the grip of the Great Depression, and with Germany unable to service the debt, an informal understanding was reached among Europe's superpowers that they should instead contribute £150 million to a special fund for the "reconstitution of Europe", with payments deferred for at least three years. This agreement, reached after weeks of intense negotiation, was hailed a major triumph for Ramsay MacDonald, the British Prime Minister, whose diplomatic skills were widely acclaimed. "The great achievement of Lausanne," said *The Times*, "is that one-sided payments from one country to another group of countries, formerly associated in war, have been abolished."

In Germany, where the Lausanne declaration was broadly welcomed but fervently condemned by Adolf Hitler, the Nazi leader, who refused to recognise the Treaty of Versailles, there was news of violence and mounting unrest. July had begun with bloody clashes between Nazis and Communists and

would end with a bitter election campaign that would see the
Nazis installed as leading party in the Reichstag, with 230
seats and almost 14 million votes. Although the election result
would confirm support for Hitler's policies, it would be insufficient to realise his dream of becoming Chancellor. "Herr
Hitler's hopes dashed forever," insisted the *Daily Telegraph*.

Elsewhere in Europe, France was in mourning after 62
men died when the *Prométhée* submarine sank during trials
off the coast of Cherbourg. Bastille Day celebrations were
cancelled in many cities, and King George V sent a message
of sympathy to French president, Albert Lebrun. In America,
the FBI was reportedly closing in on the killer of Charles
Lindbergh junior, the infant son of aviators Charles and
Anne Morrow Lindbergh, whose body had been found a
short distance from the family home in New Jersey two
months earlier. Dubbed "The Crime of the Century" and
"The Biggest Story Since the Resurrection", it would be two
years before Bruno Hauptmann, a German carpenter, was
arrested and sentenced to death by electric chair. And in
China, significant interest had been aroused by the appearance
at Shanghai's Luna Park of Song Shu-teh, purportedly the
world's tallest man at an unlikely nine feet five inches. "Song
used to be in the army," wrote *Reuters*, "but his friends
complained that he drew the enemy's fire too much for their
liking or comfort." The agency added that Song's daily meal
consisted of 24 large rice puddings, one large chicken and
two dozen eggs, and that he had a son who, at the age of four,
"had the appearance of a boy in his late teens".

The sports pages of 9 July 1932 were dominated by the
Yorkshire and England batsman Herbert Sutcliffe. At
Bradford Park Avenue the previous afternoon, the

37-year-old had become only the seventh man to score 100 first-class hundreds, following in the footsteps of Jack Hobbs, Phil Mead, Patsy Hendren, W. G. Grace, Frank Woolley and Tom Hayward. Sutcliffe's 132, compiled in a little under two hours and containing eight sixes and eight fours, was acclaimed one of his greatest innings and enabled Yorkshire to set up a mid-afternoon declaration on the final day of their County Championship game against Gloucestershire. With 15 minutes of the match remaining, the visitors had lost only three second-innings wickets and Wally Hammond was in the throes of a stubborn stand with New Zealander Ces Dacre. But two quick wickets prompted Yorkshire captain Brian Sellers to claim the extra half-hour, and Bill Bowes took the final wicket with just five balls left, yorking Tom Goddard to leave Hammond stranded on 71. George Macaulay returned five for 67 and Hedley Verity four for 54 but Sutcliffe dominated the morning headlines. Proclaiming him "The Bradman of England", the *Yorkshire Evening News* enthused: "He hit harder than ever he had done in Yorkshire cricket and – this must be an especial source of satisfaction to him – in gaining honour for himself he had a big hand in the dramatic victory gained by his side. He could not have completed his hundred hundreds in better style."

Sutcliffe had not stayed to celebrate his triumph. No sooner had the match finished than he'd dashed off to a women's cricket trial at Headingley, played on the adjacent wicket to the 10 for 10 pitch. The game between the Possibles and Probables had been arranged to assist in the selection of a Yorkshire team to meet Lancashire, and Sutcliffe had been giving the girls batting coaching. The trial ended even more dramatically than the men's match, the Probables prevailing

off the very last ball. Women's cricket was still in its infancy
… the national Women's Cricket Association had only been
formed six years earlier, and it would be another two-and-a-
half years before the first women's Test between England
and Australia. J. J. Booth, president of the Bradford Cricket
League, summed up the prevailing attitude when he told the
Yorkshire Post in July 1932: "Women's cricket as a public
exhibition is on a par with men's hat-trimming contests.
They are both pantomimic entertainments, exploited by men
to be laughed at as such women sacrifice their dignity and
their highest womanly qualities to make an inglorious
holiday." The lady cricketers coached by Sutcliffe went on
to win their Roses game. In another tight finish, they
triumphed by five wickets at Headingley with five minutes
to spare. "The players behaved in the most decorous
manner," said the *Yorkshire Post*. "Perhaps the umpires,
being men, had something to do with this."

Sutcliffe's 100th hundred sustained a purple patch that had
swept him to the top of the first-class averages. He was in the
form of his life with 1,822 runs at 79.21 – streets ahead of his
nearest challenger, Lancashire's Ernest Tyldesley, who'd
scored 1,291 runs at 67.94. During a golden spell in June,
Sutcliffe had strung together a Bradmanesque sequence of 789
runs in four innings – including a career-best 313 against Essex
at Leyton. In this game, he'd shared in a world record opening
stand of 555 with Percy Holmes, which beat the 554 amassed
by Yorkshire's John Tunnicliffe and Jack Brown against
Derbyshire at Chesterfield in 1898. The new feat was shrouded
in controversy, for after Sutcliffe threw away his wicket
thinking the record broken, he posed for a photograph with
Holmes in front of the scoreboard only for the 555 to click

back to 554. Scorebook discrepancies caused the confusion, which was only resolved when a "missing" no-ball was prudently found. Holmes called the affair "a rare to-do", while Sutcliffe expressed himself strongly on the subject. *Wisden* diplomatically stated that "some of the circumstances surrounding this Leyton achievement were not quite desirable", but added that "whether the record was or was not beaten, there can be no question that the batsmen, had they not felt assured they had beaten it, could have put on heaps more runs".

Well played, old man. Percy Holmes, left, and Herbert Sutcliffe celebrate their historic stand at Leyton one month prior to the 10 for 10 match.

Ron Deaton collection

Just as Holmes and Sutcliffe would provide an astonishing postscript to the 10 for 10 with their century stand, so Verity supplied a stunning footnote to the 555. He followed this partnership with five for eight in the first innings and five for 45 in the second to seal victory by an innings and 313 runs. Verity was again in outstanding form and he went into the historic Nottinghamshire match with 80 wickets at 15.25, including 26 in his previous three games. Verity was fifth in the national averages to Harold Larwood (77 wickets at 10.74), Kent leg-spinner "Tich" Freeman (149 at 12.65), Bill Voce (92 at 13.04) and Middlesex paceman Jack Durston (70 at 14.27). With Sutcliffe unstoppable and Verity unplayable,

Yorkshire were on a tremendous run after a terrible start to the season. The champions had won only one of their opening seven games in the 28-match programme and at one stage sat second-bottom of the table – a capital offence in the county of Wilfred Rhodes and Emmott Robinson. Woeful weather played its part; two of those games were washed out as rain lashed the country through much of May, but Lancashire won by an innings and 50 runs at Bradford and Hampshire secured their first victory over Yorkshire for 10 years with a 49-run triumph at Headingley. Yorkshire's solitary success during this period came against Somerset at Bath, where Verity took nine wickets in a game Yorkshire won by the same margin.

With hopes of a second straight title seemingly over, there had been no stopping Yorkshire thereafter; four successive away wins had laid a foundation from which they never looked back, and they welcomed Nottinghamshire on the back of a 10-match unbeaten run that comprised seven victories and three draws. In a twinkling, Yorkshire had climbed to second in the table and now looked odds-on to maintain a proud record of never having finished lower than fourth since 1911, and only twice lower than fourth since 1892. They'd closed to within 10 points of leaders Kent, who'd thrashed Northamptonshire at Tunbridge Wells the previous day in a game that produced the only other 10-wicket feat of 1932. On the opening day, Northamptonshire's off-spinning all-rounder Vallance Jupp took 10 for 127 from 39 overs only to be thrillingly upstaged by Freeman, who returned match figures of 16 for 82 to force an innings win.

Yorkshire's revival was a rousing response to those who'd doubted the champions' credentials. The club was entering its third and arguably greatest phase, with only the 1950s/1960s

combinations led by Ronnie Burnet, Vic Wilson and Brian
Close standing comparison. So strong under Lord Hawke at
the turn of the century, when they won four Championships
in five years, and again in the early 1920s, when they became
the first county to win four straight titles, Yorkshire would
win a magnificent seven Championships in the nine seasons
up to the Second World War. Masterminding their success
was a man who, like Hawke before him and Burnet in later
times, was paradoxically one of their lesser stars. Brian Sellers
was no more than a string of fairy lights compared to the
Blackpool Illuminations of Holmes and Sutcliffe, Verity and
Bowes, but he made up in motivational acumen what he
lacked in playing ability. Son of Arthur Sellers, a former
Yorkshire batsman who now chaired the club's selection
committee, Sellers junior was just 25 when he led the team on
his first-class debut against Oxford University in the opening
match of 1932. Nepotism may have played a part in his rise
through the ranks but providence helped to bring him the
captaincy; although Sellers took charge at Oxford, the official
club captain was Frank Greenwood, a useful batsman who'd
led Yorkshire to the title in 1931. However, Greenwood
played just seven times in 1932 after his father's death, which
forced him to prioritise business interests, and it fell on Sellers
to step into the breach in the days when amateurs captained
the club.

Tall and thickset, with a no-nonsense bearing, Sellers was
blessed with the appearance of authority. He looked more
like a centre-half than a cricketer, the sort who'd quickly
upend an opponent to lay down a marker for the rest of the
match. A strict disciplinarian, Sellers won respect not so
much through batting ability but approach to the game and
attitude to colleagues. He put the team's interests first and led

Yorkshire in 1932. Back row (l–r): Billy Ringrose (scorer), Hedley Verity, Frank Dennis, Bill Bowes, Arthur Rhodes, Arthur Mitchell, Bright Heyhirst (masseur). Front row (l–r): Wilf Barber, George Macaulay, Percy Holmes, Brian Sellers (captain), Herbert Sutcliffe, Maurice Leyland, Arthur Wood. (Yorkshire CCC)

from the front. Yet for all his captaincy skill, the side under his control was so talented it could probably have run itself. Yorkshire's first-choice XI – the one that played in the 10 for 10 game – was awash with class and colourful characters.

Sutcliffe spearheaded the batting and was a national hero; in Australia in 1924–25, he'd set a new record for most runs in a Test series (734) and played a key role in the Ashes wins of 1926 and 1929. A self-made batsman, with prodigious concentration, Sutcliffe possessed a heavenly hook and clinical cover drive. The epitome of sartorial elegance, he wore spotless silk shirts, Savile Row suits and scrupulously parted, shiny black hair. R. C. Robertson-Glasgow said Sutcliffe was "the sort of man who would rather miss a train than run for it, and so be seen in disorder and heard breathing heavily". Neville Cardus called him "the pin-up boy in the bedrooms of countless Yorkshire girls" and said he appeared into a dour Yorkshire team as "some Lothario might have appeared among Cromwell's Ironsides".

Holmes, eight years Sutcliffe's senior at 45, made his first-class debut before the war and was the oldest player in the Headingley match. The average age of both the Yorkshire and Nottinghamshire sides was 30, and in those days a cricketer's lifespan was longer; Wilfred Rhodes had played his last Test two years earlier, aged 52, while Jack Hobbs was still going strong in his 50th year – and scored more than half his first-class hundreds after the age of 40. Dainty and dexterous, with a full range of shots, Holmes had a sprightly demeanour and Stan Laurel grin. Cardus likened him to a "stable-boy" and said he "seemed to brush an innings, comb it, making the appropriate whistling sounds". The third great pillar of the Yorkshire batting was Maurice Leyland, a popular 31-year-old left-hander who'd been an England regular since

1928. Broad-beamed and terrier-like, Leyland could cream the cover off the ball or play a backs-to-the-wall innings of Sutcliffian concentration. Completing the top-order were Wilf "Tiddly" Barber and Arthur "Ticker" Mitchell, emerging players of contrasting stature. Barber, 31, was small, slim and technically solid, while Mitchell, 29, was tall, tenacious and physically terrifying; his menacing features, set in steel, would not have looked out of place in the East End ganglands governed by the Krays.

The polar opposite of Mitchell was Arthur Wood, a wicketkeeper whose stocky build belied a penchant for taking the ball with a somersault thrown in. Known as "Rhubarb" or "Sawdust", Wood, 33, had been first choice for four years and was regarded by Bowes as "one of the grandest little fat fellows you could ever wish to meet". Bowes, 23, was the side's youngest member and its most identifiable because he didn't conform to the stereotype of a cricketer; blond and bespectacled, with studious mien, he looked as if he'd escaped from a science lecture and that his presence on the field was a scientific experiment. Yet Bowes achieved great control from a six-foot five-inch frame and 10-yard run-up, which gave way to a perfectly synchronised, cartwheel action, and he had the ability to swing the ball late. His new-ball partner, Arthur Rhodes, was 25 and had debuted in the same fixture as Sellers at Oxford; a "Steady Eddie" sort, with straight-backed manner, Rhodes – no relation to the famous Wilfred – had the air of a dutiful policeman. The bowling unit was completed by Verity's spin partner George Macaulay, Yorkshire's leading wicket-taker in their four titles from 1922 to 1925, and one of a select band to have taken a wicket with his first ball in Test cricket, against South Africa at Cape Town in 1923 (Macaulay hit the winning run for good measure). Friendly one minute, ferocious the next, Macaulay was the sort of man who might have picked a fight with his own shadow and then immediately offered to buy it a drink. Rough-and-ready, with wafer-thin lips made for wedging Woodbines, Macaulay, 34, glared and glowered at team-mates and opponents and thought nothing of deliberately bowling beamers.

The Nottinghamshire side was similarly colourful – and none more vibrant than its charismatic captain. Arthur Carr was a loveable rogue, the sort who believed that life was a blast and who possessed the cash to pursue the philosophy. The son of a stockbroker and racehorse owner, Carr attended Sherborne, where the novelist Alec Waugh, elder brother of Evelyn, had an unrequited crush on him. Waugh made him the model for "the tremendous" Lovelace in *The Loom of Youth*, a controversial book about Waugh's schooldays which openly mentioned homosexuality. Strong and sturdy, with receding fair hair and sea-blue eyes, Carr took his cricket as grimly as he took beer gladly. He drank like a fish and smoked three packets of cigarettes a day; it wasn't unusual for him to turn up to a match still in his dinner jacket from the previous night. A combative character, who'd led England in six Tests between 1926 to 1929, Carr established a drinking culture at Trent Bridge every bit as successful as the cricketing one, and made it his job to see that Harold Larwood – his premier pace bowler – took to beer, thus enabling him to replace lost fuel. "When I have particularly wanted to get Larwood's tail up in order to get a quick wicket or two for Notts, I have seen to it that he has not wanted for a drop of beer," said Carr, who believed "you cannot be a good fast bowler on a bottle of ginger pop or a nice glass of cold water".

To judge by a return of 13 for 76 at Worcestershire two days before the 10 for 10 match, Larwood did not want for a drop or two in the New Road dressing room. His figures – which would remain the best of his career – inspired a crushing victory, Nottinghamshire's third in four Championship games. After a steady start to the season, Carr's side had climbed to third in the table, 18 points behind Yorkshire with two games in hand. But just as Yorkshire were a team on the rise, so Nottinghamshire's star was starting to wane; 1932 would be something of a watershed, a season that concluded their second great period. Dominant in the 10 years prior to the Championship's formation in 1890, when they were seven times the unofficial champions, Nottinghamshire won the title in 1907 but had to wait until 1929 to repeat the feat. It was the culmination of a successful decade under Carr, who'd also led them to runners-up places in 1922, 1923 and 1927. Now the team was ageing and in the throes of transition: from the regular side in 1929, Nottinghamshire had lost the formidable batting trio of George Gunn, Bill "Dodge" Whysall and Wilf Payton, along with pace bowler Fred Barratt, while several players – including 39-year-old Carr – were nudging 40.

The loss of Gunn and Whysall was particularly felt. Throughout the 20s, they'd formed an opening partnership to rival Holmes and Sutcliffe, sharing 40 century stands. The double-act ended in tragic fashion; in November 1930, Whysall died, aged 43, after slipping on a dance floor, cutting his elbow and contracting blood poisoning from his suede jacket. The second match of 1932 effectively ended Gunn's career; a full toss from Surrey's Alf Gover struck him on the head and he managed only three more first-class games, the last of them against the Indian tourists a week before the 10 for

10 match. Whysall's death was offset to some degree by the emergence of Walter Keeton, who'd stepped up after waiting five years for his chance. Lean and wiry, with a prominent forehead, the 27-year-old had opened with Gunn in 1931, scoring 1,233 runs at 30.07, but Gunn's departure at the age of 53 had left him suddenly as senior opener and Nottinghamshire with a significant headache: who now to pair with Keeton? Going into the Headingley game, Keeton – who played football at inside-right for Sunderland and Nottingham Forest – had had five different partners in his 13 Championship matches since the start of the season. Frank Shipston had been paired with him in the three fixtures prior to the Worcestershire game, for which Shipston was dropped, while Gunn had accompanied him twice and Joe Hardstaff junior and George Vernon Gunn once each. Hardstaff, 21, was not selected for Leeds but George Vernon Gunn, the boyishly handsome 26-year-old son of George senior, was chosen – albeit at No. 7 in a batting order that constantly changed.

Keeton's most frequent partner had been Charlie Harris, a 24-year-old in his first full season. One week after the Yorkshire match, Harris would make the opener's position his own and remain Keeton's chief ally until 1949, the duo recording 45 century stands. As it was, Harris batted No. 6 at Headingley and was the only member of the Nottinghamshire side without a first-class hundred, emphasising its strength. The only other members of the top-eight who occupied anything like a settled position were Carr, who mostly batted No. 4, and Willis Walker and Arthur Staples, fixtures at No. 3 and No. 5 respectively.

Tall and thin, with the hint of a head teacher, Walker, 39, lived in Keighley, the West Yorkshire town where he owned

Nottinghamshire in 1932. Back row (l–r): Charlie Harris, Sam Staples, Bill Voce, Joe Hardstaff junior, Arthur Staples, Harold Larwood, George Vernon Gunn. Front row (l–r): Willis Walker, Walter Keeton, Arthur Carr (captain), George Gunn senior, Ben Lilley. Inset: Frank Shipston. (Nottinghamshire CCC)

a sports shop. An elegant strokeplayer, who'd been a goal-keeper for Doncaster Rovers, Leeds City and Bradford Park Avenue, among others, he'd been a Nottinghamshire regular since the mid-1920s. Staples, 33, was another goalkeeper – for Mansfield Town and Bournemouth – and a sturdy batsman with a strong-armed drive. Round-faced and reliable, like a trusty old clock, he was a handy medium-pacer too, forming part of a four-strong attack that enabled Carr to play seven frontline batsmen plus wicketkeeper Ben Lilley. The latter, 38, was short, squat and stubby-fingered. One of the finest glove men in the land, Lilley was the unsung support to spearheads Larwood and Voce.

Larwood, 27, was the fastest and most feared bowler on the planet. Physically, he looked better suited to Lilley's trade than actually propelling the missiles himself. Just five foot seven and a half inches tall, Larwood weighed less than 11 stone but was strong from gruelling shifts as a miner in the days when it was said all Nottinghamshire had to do to find a fast bowler was whistle down the nearest pit. Larwood, who'd made his Test debut under Carr in 1926, had topped the first-class averages in three of the previous five seasons and would do so again in 1932 – and for a final time in 1936. Voce, another ex-miner, was the youngest player in the Headingley game at 22 but already in his sixth season; he'd headed Nottinghamshire's 1929 Championship-winning averages and taken the most wickets (23) of anyone on the 1930–31 tour of South Africa. Chubby-cheeked and curly-haired, Voce was effectively Verity in reverse; he'd started out as a left-arm spinner before converting to left-arm fast. Nottinghamshire's line-up for Leeds was completed by 39-year-old Sam Staples, elder brother of Arthur and an amiable, dimple-cheeked off-spinner with a shuffling run-up.

Skilled at sealing an end while Larwood and Voce rested, Staples made three Test appearances on the 1927–28 tour of South Africa.

Sam Staples and Carr were the only survivors from Nottinghamshire's previous visit to Headingley in 1923, when Staples's match figures of 10 for 82 underpinned a thrilling three-run victory – Nottinghamshire's solitary success in their seven trips to Leeds. Yorkshire had four survivors from that game – Holmes, Sutcliffe, Leyland and Macaulay – and although the sides were due to have met at Headingley in 1926, the match was washed out.

Events surrounding the previous Championship meeting between the clubs in Yorkshire, at Bramall Lane in July 1931, were notable and felt by many to have cost Nottinghamshire the title that Yorkshire secured. As George Vernon Gunn set off to the game with several team-mates,

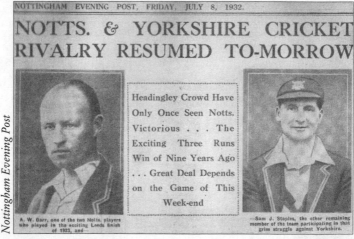

Nottingham Evening Post

NOTTINGHAM EVENING POST, FRIDAY, JULY 8, 1932.

NOTTS. & YORKSHIRE CRICKET RIVALRY RESUMED TO-MORROW

Headingley Crowd Have Only Once Seen Notts. Victorious . . . The Exciting Three Runs Win of Nine Years Ago . . . Great Deal Depends on the Game of This Week-end

A. W. Carr, one of the two Notts. players who played in the exciting Leeds finish of 1923, and—

—Sam J. Staples, the other remaining member of the team participating in that grim struggle against Yorkshire.

Setting the scene for a game that would go down in cricket history.

he hit Larwood's car side-on in a smash on Nottingham's Loughborough Road, injuring himself, Larwood and Sam Staples, Larwood's passenger, all of whom missed the match. Although Nottinghamshire emerged with a useful draw, they were thumped a week later in the return at Trent Bridge after the injured Voce joined the casualty list. Having gone into the game at Bramall Lane three points clear at the top with a match in hand, Nottinghamshire lost their way at a vital time and finished fifth. The 1932 Leeds fixture – the 99th meeting in first-class cricket between the clubs in a series Yorkshire led 35–16 with 47 draws – was billed as once more having a vital bearing on the title race. The *Nottingham Evening Post*, while praising Nottinghamshire's win at Worcestershire, stressed: "It is this weekend a case of now or never for Notts in respect of the Championship race", adding that Carr's men could only take heart from their victory over the "Sauce County".

4

A Cautious Opening

The Headingley ground was never picturesque but, today, even what little beauty it ever possessed was limited by the spectacle of workmen engaging in reconstructing the Leeds Rugby Football Club stand, which was destroyed by fire.

So proclaimed the *Nottingham Evening Post* in its opening dispatch from the 10 for 10 game. It highlighted the game's most incongruous aspect – it unfolded to the backdrop of a building site. The double-fronted stand, which faced the rugby

Yorkshire Evening Post

This grainy image from day one shows the unsightly backdrop to cricket's most stunning bowling performance. Verity was bowling from this Rugby Stand end when he took 10 for 10 later in the match.

field one way and the cricket pitch the other, was consumed by fire some three months earlier, and in a rare image taken of the historic match, a new structure is under fledgling construction, while the scene is one of chaotic disorder. A cement mixer is situated close to the boundary, like a rotund fielder stationed for a catch, and planks are scattered in random fashion, like cricket bats strewn on a dressing room floor. Hedley Verity's feat deserved heavenly surroundings, but the reality could hardly have been more different.

The fire broke out 10 minutes into a rugby league game between Leeds and Halifax on Good Friday 1932. Spectators fled for the sanctuary of the pitch as the blaze developed with terrifying speed. Although the stand held over 2,000, only one minor injury was reported – a woman sprained her ankle in the sprint for safety. Otherwise, ambulance crews treated only a handful of women who'd fainted. "At first, spectators in the stand among the crowd of more than 17,000 did not realise the seriousness of the trouble," said the *Yorkshire Post*. "Only when smoke began to rise up through the wooden planks in the floor did the gravity of the situation become clear to the masses." The cricket pavilion almost burned down too. "The two bays nearest the pavilion (which is separated from the stand by a gangway of a couple of yards) were a mass of flames," reported the *Post*. "There was a rush to remove the cricket equipment of the members of the Yorkshire team who, in recent weeks, had been practising at Headingley. The pavilion was saved, and about this time it appeared that the brigade would save the main part of the stand, but the roof of the cricket stand, which was built high over the football stand, caught, and in a matter of minutes the fire, driven by the wind, had run the length of it. This part of the blaze was spectacular."

It took two hours to control the flames. The stand, which held 2,600 on the rugby side and 1,000 on the cricket side, was destroyed apart from two bays. The cause of the fire was never established but police suspected a discarded cigarette. The damage was put at £20,000 – and the rebuilt structure still stands.

It was against this bizarre background of building work and general commotion that Brian Sellers and Arthur Carr strode out for the toss on the morning of Saturday 9 July 1932. The day was cloudy and already warm, with just a light south-westerly breeze. Carr guessed correctly and, on what *The Times* called "a perfect pitch", chose to bat. It was "a batsman's wicket from the start", insisted the *Yorkshire Post*. Yorkshire were unchanged following their win over Gloucestershire but Nottinghamshire showed one alteration to the side that beat Worcestershire. Frank Shipston replaced the out-of-sorts Joe Hardstaff junior, whose previous three innings had been 0, 1 and 2. In front of a 4,000 crowd, Shipston and Walter Keeton opened the innings to "the discordant noise of concrete mixers". Bill Bowes took the new ball from the Kirkstall Lane end and immediately attacked with five slips – George Macaulay, Herbert Sutcliffe, Arthur Rhodes, Verity and Percy Holmes.

Verity could not have begun his famous match in more fateful fashion: Shipston had yet to score when he edged an away-swinger from Bowes to fourth slip, where Verity spilled a low opportunity. Sutcliffe was also slumbering in the slips. Perhaps drained mentally after his 100th hundred, and his evening coaching the Yorkshire women, he dropped Keeton at second slip off Bowes when the batsman had four and the total was 10. It was tough luck on Bowes, whose

Yorkshire Evening Post

A rare action shot from the match as Nottinghamshire's Walter Keeton is bowled by Arthur Rhodes, even though the bails are still on the stumps.

bowling, according to *The Times*, had "the illusion rather than the reality of pace". Instead, it was Bowes's opening partner, Rhodes, who made the breakthrough – and in circumstances that caused curiosity. When Keeton had nine and the total was 15, Rhodes – bringing the ball back towards three short-legs – drew an inside-edge that saw the ball lightly graze the top of off stump. Although the three stumps remained intact, the impact caused the leg bail to pop out of its groove on the middle stump, even though it remained in its groove on the leg stump.

Wicketkeeper Arthur Wood alerted square-leg umpire Bill Reeves, a former Essex medium-pace bowler who "surveyed the scene with great enthusiasm". Dry and droll, with angular features, Reeves, 57, was a character, once telling a batsman who protested that he wasn't out to "look in the paper tomorrow morning" and a bowler who kept

Tony Debenham/Iain Taylor

Umpires Bill Reeves, left, and Harry Baldwin.

asking for lbw, "there's only one man who appeals more than you – and that's Doctor Barnardo". Reeves consulted at length with fellow official Harry Baldwin, a 39-year-old ex-Surrey batsman standing in only his 13th Championship game, and a man who crouched so low at the stumps that he looked like a slipped disc waiting to happen. Acting under a new directive that said the bails no longer had to fall to ground for a batsman to be out, they pronounced Keeton bowled – a decision that confused many spectators unable to see from a distance what happened.

The incident was in comical contrast to one that had taken place in Yorkshire's match against Surrey at Sheffield the previous week, when there'd been no problem with the bails failing to come out of their grooves for the simple reason that Surrey wicketkeeper Edward Brooks kept knocking them off for no obvious reason. The Yorkshire cricket writer A. W. Pullin bemoaned: "Brooks' antics caused amusement at first to onlookers, but this feeling subsequently changed to resentment, which was expressed with the emphasis which the 'grinders' on the Bramall Lane are famous. On very many occasions, almost in every over, in fact, Brooks took the ball and swept off the bails practically in one action. As a rule, the striker had a foot well within his crease, and the fact that there was not a single case of stumping in the innings (I refer to Yorkshire's first essay) is sufficient to show the futility of the stumper's activities. The number of times the bails had to be replaced was altogether abnormal, and when it is added that one of the umpires has an artificial leg, the inconvenience, indeed, the annoyance, caused will be realised."

Keeton was replaced by Willis Walker, who'd hit 92 when the sides met at Sheffield the previous year and top-scored in both innings of the return match at Trent Bridge. His form in 1932 had been ordinary; Walker had managed two centuries in 24 innings and not much besides. Walker and Shipston took the total to 31 before Sellers made a double change after 55 minutes, bringing on Verity at the Rugby Stand end and Macaulay at the Kirkstall Lane side. It didn't take long for Macaulay to strike; with the score on 35, Shipston played back and outside the line to the off-spinner's quicker ball and lost his off stump.

Loud cheers now greeted Carr's arrival, reflecting his love for playing big shots. But the captain was having a desperately poor season; he'd managed only one half-century in 23 innings and looked every inch the lumbering veteran. Nor were his surroundings likely to inspire him; on his previous visit in 1926, when he'd led England against Australia, Carr dropped Charles Macartney in the first over after controversially putting the tourists into bat, Macartney racing to a century before lunch. Although England emerged with a draw – thanks, in no small part, to Macaulay, who top-scored from No. 10 with 76 in the first innings – Carr was made a scapegoat and relieved of the captaincy after the next Test at Old Trafford, where he fell ill with tonsillitis, which some suspected was actually a hangover.

Carr defended stoically for 15 minutes against Macaulay and Verity before perishing to his first attacking shot; he connected cleanly with an attempted straight six off Verity but was brilliantly caught by Wilf Barber, who ran 20 yards from wide long-on to snatch the ball in front of the sightscreen. Carr's dismissal for a duck to the final ball of Verity's fifth over left Nottinghamshire 40 for three and in need of a sizeable score from Arthur Staples, whose recent form had led to calls for his consideration for the tour to Australia. Staples got off the mark first ball with a three to square-leg off Macaulay but became hopelessly bogged down and had not added to his tally when, 20 minutes later, Macaulay knocked back his middle stump with another quicker delivery as the visitors slumped to 46 for four. Nottinghamshire lurched into lunch on 61 for four (Walker 34, Charlie Harris 2, Verity 1 for 14 from 13 overs), their struggles in perfect conditions highlighted by the fact they did not hit a boundary during the session.

A crowd that had mushroomed during the morning could only hope for better after the break, when 16,000 would fill the ground to give Yorkshire their largest gate of the season. Not only was the meeting between the Championship's second and third-placed teams an attractive draw, but

Yorkshire Evening Post

*The only other known action photograph from the 10 for 10 fixture as
Arthur Staples is bowled by George Macaulay in the Nottinghamshire
first innings.*

county cricket in the 1930s was much more popular than it
is today; Yorkshire's average daily attendance during the
decade was around 8,000, while the club often pulled gates
of 15,000-plus for important matches. With Test cricket
holding scarcity value, and with no television to tempt
away spectators, the Championship held considerable
significance, with the players themselves widely esteemed.
To put that 16,000 figure into context, it was only a few
hundred less than watched the opening day of the last
Headingley Ashes Test in 2009. In the 1930s, people flocked
to the ground on trams and trains, buses and bicycles, or
simply walked from miles around. Enthusiasm for the game
flew in the face of the economic climate, with the Great

Depression – triggered by the Wall Street crash of 1929 – causing hardship for many working-class families. In northern cities such as Leeds, unemployed men hung around on street corners, among them those who'd returned from the First World War with broken bodies and broken spirits, while women struggled on war widow's pensions, many relying on soup kitchens for food and hand-me-down clothes for their children. In Leeds, unemployment in June 1932 alone rose by 2,004 to 27,092, while 60 miles north in Stockton-on-Tees, a staggering 70 per cent of the workforce was jobless. Cricket was a means of escape at a time of fewer competing entertainments; it was also comparatively affordable. Admission to the Yorkshire-Nottinghamshire match ranged from 1s 6d for adults (around £2.50 today) to 2s 4d (around £4 today), with concessions for children and OAPs. Of the 16,000 who saw the first day, 9,656 paid, earning Yorkshire £552 (about £18,500 today). The rest were members who normally watched from the Rugby Stand but, due to the building work, were temporarily moved to the 2s 4d seats. This deprived non-members of the chance to sit in those better seats – an unavoidable inconvenience that cut no ice with someone called "Londoner", who complained to the *Yorkshire Evening Post*.

> *Sir,*
> *Some thousands of cricket enthusiasts visited the ground for the Notts match with the intention of occupying the 2s 4d seats. Upon arriving at the gate, they found that those seats had been reserved for the use of members only, owing to the new stand being erected on the space usually occupied by members.*

The consequence was that only the 1s 6d portion was
available for people who would willingly have paid 2s 4d,
or even more. There was no notice in the newspapers to
that effect, nor posters near the gates.
It is pleasing to note that the new stand is progressing and
no doubt before next season the pavilion will receive a
coat of paint. At present it is the unanimous opinion that
the shabbiest county cricket ground is at Headingley.

Despite "Londoner's" criticisms, the Leeds venue was
arguably more attractive than it is today, and certainly more
arboreal and expansive. Although the building work marred
it in 1932, the ground had a knot of elm trees at the Kirkstall
Lane end, which is nowadays served by the Carnegie
Pavilion, and a bowling green behind the exposed area
presently occupied by the sprawling East Stand. The old
pavilion, with its dark-brown brickwork and gleaming
white railings, was the only proper stand as such and
possessed two towers at each end – one of which housed the
press, the other the scorers (in this case, the Yorkshire scorer
Billy Ringrose and his Nottinghamshire counterpart Jack
Carlin). The concrete cycle track, which in those days
enabled freedom of movement all round the ground, added
to a feeling of space largely shattered by contemporary
structures. Photographs of the period show Headingley to
be, if not quite a good-looking ground, then at least one
tastefully arranged and with less of a slapdash feel than it has
now – as if, in the words of former *Yorkshire Post* cricket
correspondent Rob Mills, "it has been put together by a
hyperactive seven-year-old with a few Lego bricks left
over". Those photographs show crowds immaculately
ordered in lines and rows, with barely a Homburg out of

place, and in subdued rather than showy fashions. In those austere times, sombre hues were de rigueur and sunnier colours in short supply. Schoolboys watched in dark colours too, the luckier ones forming a guard of honour to clap the players on and off the field.

In an arrangement between Yorkshire and the building contractor, the Leeds-based William Airey and Sons, work on the Rugby Stand stopped when the bowling was from that end and continued when the action resumed from the Kirkstall Lane side. It was in front of the cement mixers and clutter, the wooden planks and workmen, that Nottingham-shire lost their fifth wicket on 67 just after lunch. Bowes, recalled to the attack with Rhodes, banged in a bouncer at Walker, who top-edged a hook to Barber on the long-leg boundary next to the rubble. Walker had added only two to his lunchtime score but, according to the *Yorkshire Evening Post*, had "served his side faithfully in trying circumstances". It should have been 67 for six but Bowes missed George Vernon Gunn in the same over before he'd scored. The ball was short and Gunn, shaping to pull, spliced in the air, Bowes falling over as he charged down the wicket to try to take the catch. Ivan Sharpe, of the *Sunday Chronicle*, was particularly critical of Bowes's blunder, insisting it proved England could not afford to take both him and Frank Woolley, the veteran Kent batsman, to Australia that winter – at least not to play in the same side. "D. R. Jardine would have a prize problem in setting his field if he had to hide both Woolley and Bowes," stated Sharpe. In the end, Bowes would make the trip but Woolley would not. Bowes's fielding was as ridiculed as his bowling was revered. For Yorkshire, he stood at mid-on and barely moved a muscle.

On Sellers's orders, it was understood that to save Bowes's legs, and most probably his blushes, it was somebody else's job to chase the ball and throw it in. Bowes was only expected to stop or catch it if it went straight at him. Similarly, if Bowes, the archetypal No. 11, lingered at the crease and wasted time, it was his partner's duty to run him out, which partly explained why he took more first-class wickets (1,639) than he scored runs (1,531).

Bowes was in the side to take wickets and he'd helped put Yorkshire into a commanding position against their title rivals. However, as cloud gave way to afternoon sunshine, and as the temperature climbed to 82 degrees, his botched attempt to catch Gunn sparked a momentum shift as the innings underwent slow reconstruction. Twenty minutes into the session, Harris finally recorded the first boundary of the match, glancing Bowes just wide of Barber at long leg, the *Nottingham Guardian* remarking that "the spectators were almost too surprised to cheer". But Nottinghamshire sought to recover through defensive means, a tactic that angered the belligerent Bowes, who tried to upset the batsmen with bouncers. Just over one month later, Bowes would employ the same strategy against Surrey's Jack Hobbs at The Oval, in the process attracting fierce criticism from former Middlesex batsman "Plum" Warner, whose contention in the *Morning Post* that it was "not cricket" would be thrown back at him after he returned from co-managing the Bodyline tour. Tensions between Bowes and Hobbs – paradoxically two of cricket's nicest men – would boil over when Hobbs walked down the pitch after one bouncer to pat a spot near the bowler's stumps. Egged on by George Macaulay, Bowes would respond with an even shorter delivery, Hobbs this time reacting by walking past the stumps altogether and patting down a spot in the bowler's run-up. Later, Macaulay would fling two beamers at Surrey captain Douglas Jardine, who'd duck them disdainfully.

Bowes's bouncers at Leeds were primarily designed to hurry up Harris, one of cricket's most exasperating players. Like George Gunn senior, Harris was renowned for blocking bad balls and belting blameless deliveries to the boundary; like Gunn senior too, his batting reflected his quirky personality. Stories of Harris's foibles abound; one of his favourite whims was to provide a running commentary of his innings as he imagined it might appear in the papers. "Harris was in a very dour mood today," he might say, "and certainly not at his best." Naturally funny, which belied a somewhat challenging facial appearance, Harris once emerged from the pavilion in bad light carrying a candle and walked to the scoreboard instead of the wicket; sometimes he took out his false teeth and laid them on the ground while fielding. Best of all, story goes that he once ended up in hospital after dislocating his shoulder and was moaning and groaning as they tried to put it back. Eventually, the nurse lost patience: "Look, there's a woman downstairs who's just had twins and she's making far less noise than you." "Ah yes," said Harris, "but are they trying to put them back?"

Gunn was a more conventional character and the least cele-brated of the family dynasty. As well as having a father *Wisden* called "one of the cricketing marvels of the age", George Vernon's uncle was John Gunn, the only Nottinghamshire player to score more than 20,000 runs and take over 1,000 wickets, while his great uncle was Billy Gunn, who enjoyed prodigious partnerships with Arthur

Shrewsbury in the 19th century. Gunn junior was not in the same talent bracket but was still a useful county pro; the previous year, he'd scored his maiden century against Warwickshire at Edgbaston, George Gunn senior also hitting a hundred in the only instance of a father and son making a three-figure score in the same Championship innings. After a sticky patch in 1932, Gunn junior had returned to form with 86 in the win against Worcestershire two days earlier, and now he capitalised on Bowes's failure to catch him at Leeds by helping Harris draw the sting from the attack and, as a consequence, the fun from the day. Both men carried caution to the nth degree against Verity, who again followed Rhodes at the Rugby Stand end. There was no spin or bounce in the pitch but Verity was patient and persevering and a combination of his accuracy and Nottinghamshire's apathy resulted in a sober stalemate for the crowd. Only once did Gunn throw caution to the wind, swatting Verity over long-on towards the pavilion to register the second four of the innings after three hours' play. Otherwise, spectators tired of the respect the batsmen showed to Verity and ironically applauded Harris when he pushed out a straight dead bat to ball after ball.

Keen to fashion a much-needed breakthrough, Sellers turned to Maurice Leyland, a part-time left-arm spinner who replaced Verity at 120 for five after Verity's second spell of 11 overs for 12 runs. It was a masterstroke, Leyland striking with his fifth ball to have Harris lbw for 35, ending a stand of 53. It was not Leyland who appealed but wicketkeeper Wood, who then missed a simple stumping when Leyland was immediately withdrawn and replaced again by Verity. Gunn, on 26, was lured out of his ground only for Wood to make what the *Sunday Chronicle* termed "a Saturday afternoon mess of the chance". Verity's reaction was typically restrained; he never got mad if a chance went begging. "If you dropped a catch off him he just smiled," remembered the former Yorkshire and England batsman Len Hutton. "I never saw him angry or even agitated at a turn of events in a game. He had a remarkable temperament." Moments before tea, Macaulay dropped Ben Lilley off his own bowling, Nottinghamshire dining on 148 for six (Gunn 26, Lilley 19).

Verity got Gunn soon after the break, bowling him for 31 to leave the visitors 159 for seven. It heralded the only hitting of the day as Harold Larwood joined Lilley. Larwood was hardly the worst No. 9; he had three first-class hundreds to his name, the highest an innings of 102 not out against Sussex at Trent Bridge the previous year. In the lull of late afternoon, Larwood immediately set about the bowling – but not before he'd set about his partner. Larwood's first aggressive shot was a searing straight drive off Rhodes that sent Lilley's bat flying out of his hands as he desperately took evasive action, the sort of grim spectacle Larwood normally produced with the ball. The fast bowler followed up by straight-driving Rhodes for four – this time missing the ducking Lilley – and launching Verity for a straight six into the excavations for the new stand, the ball ricocheting among the wooden planks and causing a stoppage while it was retrieved. Once again, Verity was unmoved. As Bowes wrote, "If you saw nothing but his poker face it would be impossible to tell whether his ball had been knocked for six or had spreadeagled the stumps."

Not many knocked Verity's ball for six ... Frank Woolley once did so four times during an incredible innings of 188 out of 296 for four at Bradford, bringing Verity back down to earth a fortnight after his 10 for 36. Hugh Bartlett, the Sussex batsman, smashed him for six sixes in two overs on his way to

94 during a game at Headingley in 1938. However, considering that slow bowlers are liable to such punishment, Verity was rarely taken apart. The most famous assault on him came at Sheffield in 1935, when the South African wicketkeeper Jock Cameron thumped him for 30 in one over – three fours followed by three sixes as Verity deliberately tossed the ball up. It sparked one of cricket's most celebrated quips. As Cameron peppered the Bramall Lane boundary, Arthur Wood called out, "Go on, Hedley, you have him in two minds. He doesn't know whether to hit you for four or six."

As Larwood made a mockery of earlier tardiness, Nottinghamshire's total raced to 200. In those days, a fielding team were entitled to a new ball after 200 runs had been scored, and having bowled unchanged since tea with limited success, Verity now experimented with four overs of medium-paced swingers to four short-legs, reprising his days in Lancashire League cricket. The tactic stifled Larwood but did not shift him, and after Verity's third and final spell brought one for 38 from 17 overs, Sellers again summoned up Leyland. As he'd shown by dismissing Harris before tea, Leyland was a handy partnership-breaker, who'd be good enough to take 466 first-class wickets at 29.31. J. M. Kilburn, who joined the *Yorkshire Post* as cricket correspondent two years after the 10 for 10 game, said, "Leyland's bowling is mostly a joke, but it is an extremely practical joke", even if the impression is of "seaside holiday bowling where a spade is the bat and the wicket a stanchion of the pier". Leyland made no claim for his second string but did insist he invented the term "Chinaman", the slow left-armer's ball that spins from off to leg. The derivation is mostly attributed to an incident during the Old Trafford Test of 1933 between

England and West Indies. When England batsman Walter Robins was stumped off left-arm spinner Ellis "Puss" Achong, a Trinidadian of Chinese ancestry, he is said to have walked off grumbling, "Fancy being done by a bloody Chinaman." Learie Constantine, fielding nearby, purportedly enquired, "Do you mean the bowler or the ball?" However, Leyland was adamant that he coined the term, a claim backed up by the fact that in the 1920s Yorkshire's Roy Kilner would often urge his captain, if a wicket was overdue, "Put Maurice on to bowl some of those Chinese things." Kilner, who'd been expected to take Wilfred Rhodes's place as left-arm spinner but for his death from enteric fever in 1928, would add, "It's foreign stuff – and you can't call it anything else."

Whatever it was, and whoever coined it, Leyland's wiles were too much for Nottinghamshire, who subsided swiftly in the evening shadows. At 233, Larwood lashed out and was bowled for 48, ending what the *Leeds Mercury* called "a capital little innings full of clean, crisp driving" and a stand of 74 with Lilley. Leyland wrapped up the innings by bowling Bill Voce and Sam Staples for ducks to finish with four for 14 from 8.2 overs, the last three wickets for no runs in eight balls. Nottinghamshire were all out at 6.20 for 234 (Lilley 46 not out) and there was no time to start the Yorkshire reply. Leyland, who'd been heavily quoted in the newspapers that day after the death of former Warwickshire and England fast bowler Harry Howell, whose 10 for 51 against Yorkshire at Edgbaston in 1923 he'd called "the best piece of bowling I have seen", and which is still the only 10-fer against Yorkshire in the Championship, was now heavily praised. The *Yorkshire Post* said: "The success of the extraordinarily mixed material he used to confound the Notts batsmen was, perhaps, the outstanding feature on a day when the bat, contrary to expectations, was always struggling against the ball." Verity, whom one writer said "was never the equal of Leyland", finished with two for 64 from 41 overs. Nottinghamshire faced 132.2 overs for a dilatory run-rate of 1.7.

Elsewhere, slow scoring was also a feature at the Bath Festival, where fourth-bottom Glamorgan crawled to 110 in 86 overs before seventh-bottom Somerset replied with 141 for three. Ditto in the mid-table meeting at Southampton, where Hampshire made 120 in 87.4 overs against Middlesex, who reached 95 for two. In contrast, runs flowed at Old Trafford, where Lancashire were 442 for five against the Indian tourists (Ernest Tyldesley 196); at Chesterfield, where lower mid-table Derbyshire were 393 for five against lowly Essex (Garnet Lee 101 not out), and at Blackheath, where Freddie Brown struck 168 of mid-table Surrey's 345 against leaders Kent, who reached 78 for one. Otherwise, wickets tumbled steadily: 20 at Northampton, where the third-bottom home team scored 105 in reply to bottom club Gloucestershire's 228; 17 at Kidderminster, where fifth-placed Sussex were 158 for seven after dismissing second-bottom Worcestershire for 192, and 14 at Coventry, where mid-table Leicestershire were 87 for four in reply to struggling Warwickshire's 222.

For the players and supporters of Yorkshire and Nottinghamshire, a rest day now followed, along with a choice of entertainments that Saturday evening. Leeds Hippodrome was showing *Whose Baby Are You?* – "a screamingly funny revue featuring Jimmy James"; Leeds Coliseum was screening *Charlie Chan's Chance*, starring Warner Oland, while The New Manor had Lon Chaney, aka

"The Man of a Thousand Faces", in *The Hunchback of Notre Dame*. Local nightspots swayed to such numbers as "Ain't Misbehavin'" and "Goodnight, Sweetheart", while Sir Barry Jackson, founder of the Birmingham Repertory Theatre, was holding court at Leeds Eyebrow Club with his meditations on the Malvern Festival. But if the cinema, popular music or theatrical reflections were not to one's palate, there was always the option of tuning into North Regional Radio, frequency 479.2, where "the great George Hirst" was to make a special appeal on behalf of Huddersfield Royal Infirmary followed by "one or two cricketing reminiscences".

Stormy Weather

THE WRONG KIND OF CRICKET
Notts in the doldrums
3 for 0 finish by Leyland

NOTTS "TAIL" TO THE RESCUE
All-day struggle at 40 runs an hour
Failure of the "reliables"

NOTTS COULD HAVE DONE WITH GEORGE GUNN
"Slow motion" in the vital Yorkshire game
No excitement, and not a laugh until Larwood goes in!

The newspaper headlines said it all following the start to the fixture at Headingley. Writers who'd commend the thrilling finish initially condemned the tedious beginning, which offered no sign of the drama to follow. While most correspondents said Yorkshire bowled well, particularly Maurice Leyland with his "Chinese" concoctions, the general feeling was the catching had been ropy and the Nottinghamshire batting positively dopey. For Arthur Carr and the visiting players, the column inches made for as uncomfortable reading as their own batting made for uninteresting viewing. Frank Stainton, of the *Leeds Mercury*, felt Nottinghamshire "sinned against a glorious summer's day" and said it had been "utter boredom for a magnificent crowd of 16,000 spectators". Corney, of the *Nottingham Journal*, said he could "scarcely believe Notts could carry patience so far" and described it as "tortoise cricket". Corney added: "Cricket is a strange game. On the same ground two years ago, I believe Bradman made a century before lunch all by himself. And that was in a Test match!" Some of the strongest criticism came from Frederick Elam, a batsman who'd played briefly for Yorkshire at the turn of the century. In his *Yorkshire Evening Post* column, Elam said he'd gone to Headingley after reading of the thrilling win against Gloucestershire at Bradford in the hope there might be "something similar" only to return home "a disappointed and disillusioned man". He went on: "There were one or two thrills at first, that of the partially-dislodged bail being unique in my experience, and another at the end, when Maurice Leyland's 'dollies' polished off the last three batsmen in about 10 minutes. In between these two extremes all the rest was deadly dull. The Notts batsmen were there, not to score runs, but to wear down the bowling. Runs were merely incidental and hardly seemed to be an important part of the game." Elam said the pitch gave the bowlers "not the least assistance" and thought the outfield "as fast as a billiard table". He added that the vast crowd was the "quietest" of the season. "Like the Yorkshire bowlers, they took their medicine – and it was nasty stuff – with hardly a murmur. Imagination boggles at what would have been said at Bramall Lane. Brighter cricket! When shall we get it if the third county in the Championship table can send us to sleep like this?"

Amid the chorus of condemnation, only *The Times* took a contrary view. "Such a rate of scoring – 234 runs in six hours – argues a dull day's cricket, but as a matter of fact the

Yorkshire out-cricket was so aggressive and militant and the batsmen had to fight so hard for their runs that there was barely a dull minute from beginning to end."

Notwithstanding the consensus the cricket was prosaic, some 5,000 spectators were present for the start of day two – a beautifully sunny Monday morning. The temporary members' enclosure was already packed, and by noon the seats at the Kirkstall Lane end would all be taken, the crowd eventually climbing to 14,000. It was the school holidays and, in those days, children were allowed to sit on the grass beside the boundary, savouring their sandwiches and bottles of pop in proximity to heroes like Hedley Verity. The man himself would oblige autograph hunters with a cheerful smile and a careful signature, recognising such kindness would make their day and remain imprinted on their memories for life. According to the *Nottingham Guardian*, there was "quite a Test match atmosphere" inside the ground as the clock ticked down to the 11.30 start. There was "an audible hum of expectant chatter" and "a sea of cloth caps and broad brimmed hats". Folk were snapping up 2d score-cards, which advertised everything from lemonade to car insurance, while cushion sellers were in high demand, their products softening the rough wooden benches. Newspaper vendors were hard at work too, moving among the mounting masses with the early edition of the *Yorkshire Evening Post*, which led on a heart-rending story from Europe.

In the grey light of dawn, the shadow of death stalked through the deserted streets of the little Romanian town of Isaccea, and struck cold fear to the hearts of the inhabitants. Twenty-five escaped lepers had invaded the town. During the night, a group of starving men, ridden with the "grey plague", and in the last stages of this most dreadful disease, broke out of the Tichilesti leper station and made for the lights of the unsuspecting town. They carried death by inches in their hands. The news of the leper invasion spread like wildfire, and very soon the whole town was panic-stricken. All the inhabitants locked and barricaded their doors, and white faces peered from behind shutters on the terrible band of death. The lepers were in an appalling condition. Wearing the rags of their isolation uniforms, they dragged their tired feet through the deserted streets, hammered on the closed doors, and cried for food. At last a cordon of police was drawn round them, and their plight was explained. It appeared that the leper station had been without food or money for several weeks. The station doctor had left for Bucharest ten days before to get help, but he had never returned. Dying of thirst and starvation, twenty-five of the lepers broke out of the compound and made for Isaccea in search of food. The police at once instituted isolation measures. A supply of food and money was collected from the terrified inhabitants, and in the evening the ghastly band was escorted back to the station under a heavy guard. The dying men looked for the last time on the world they were about to leave, and then withdrew within the grey walls of the terrible prison where fate had ordained that they should spend their lives – waiting for a terrible death by inches.

As well as the import of the fixture at Headingley, the sun-soaked weather and effect of the holidays, there was another reason for the sizeable crowd – the presence of

Nottinghamshire duo Harold Larwood and Bill Voce. As the players and umpires took to the field, greeted by "a surge of enthusiastic applause", Larwood went to the Kirkstall Lane end and began to pace out his 20-yard run. Facing him was the backdrop of a building site that had changed significantly since Saturday's play. Not only were some of the stand's high girders now in place, but a canvas screen some 50 yards long had been erected to cover the sight of the workmen, who were once more toiling in 80-degree temperatures. Amid the clank of steel and churn of cement mixers, Larwood hared down the hill to bowl the opening ball of the Yorkshire reply. It was devastatingly quick and missed Percy Holmes's off stump by a whisker, prompting a collective gasp from the crowd. Holmes jammed down on the second delivery and squirted it out to leg for a single. It brought Herbert Sutcliffe on strike for his first innings after his 100th hundred.

Sutcliffe had got to the ground early that morning, keen for a spot of extra practice. After checking the field in stately fashion, like a monarch inspecting the Household Division, he settled down to face his first ball. Larwood put every ounce of effort into it and Sutcliffe edged a delivery that pitched a foot outside off stump into the bucket hands of Voce at third slip. At once the crowd was stunned into silence. Sutcliffe walked diagonally past Voce and back to the pavilion after suffering the rarity of a golden duck. The *Yorkshire Post* felt Sutcliffe "put out a defensive bat which looked strangely uncertain", while the *Yorkshire Evening News* insisted it was "almost incredible to think that Sutcliffe could be dismissed without scoring, and still more so that it should happen first ball. However, it is the unexpected that gives cricket its charm, and that is all we need to say about it." Above the horrified hush of home supporters, the *Nottingham Guardian* said a lone voice cried out: "Good old Harold!"

Sutcliffe invariably followed the same routine after being dismissed. He'd have a wash, a rub down, and dress methodically before carefully producing his leather writing case. As the cricket unfolded, he'd sit in a quiet corner of the dressing room and attend to letters in immaculate hand. Occasionally, he'd look up and ask: "How are we doing?" The answer, on this occasion, would not have been favourable, for when the score had reached 15 Yorkshire lost Arthur Mitchell, their No. 3, when Larwood dealt him a sickening blow. Mitchell, who'd made an unbeaten 177 to set up the victory over Gloucestershire three days earlier, was trying to dodge a bouncer when the ball hit the back of his right hand with "a resounding crack". He immediately dropped his bat and was forced to retire. Bright Heyhirst, the Yorkshire masseur, quickly reported that nothing was broken but said the nerves in Mitchell's fingers were so deadened he couldn't even feel the bat, let alone grip it.

In those days, batsmen had scant protection against quicker bowlers. There were no helmets or grilles in the 1930s, while pads and gloves were pitifully flimsy. Some of Larwood's opponents resorted to shoving bath towels down their trousers as makeshift thigh pads or under their shirts as improvised rib guards. It was like trying to cushion a sub-machine gun. Despite his relatively tiny frame, Larwood touched speeds of 100mph. In the 30s, bowlers could also drag their back foot before releasing the ball, provided part of the foot landed behind the stumps, meaning Larwood could get a yard or two closer to the batsman,

"The Silent Killer": Harold Larwood in full flow.

who had less time to react than modern players facing similar speeds. So smooth and soundless was his lightning run-up, the umpire Frank Chester once claimed he didn't realise Larwood had come on to bowl until he was right beside him. Joe Hardstaff junior nicknamed his team-mate "The Silent Killer" and said he was at his lethal best when you couldn't hear him running in at all.

With hindsight, it is remarkable that "The Silent Killer" did not indeed kill anyone given the vulnerability of batsmen in a helmet-free era. Fractures and flesh wounds were common in fixtures involving Nottinghamshire – particularly in the summer of 1932. Only a week before injuring Mitchell at Headingley, Larwood had drawn blood from the left cheek of Indian tail-ender Joginder Singh during the

Trent Bridge tour match, causing a trip to hospital. Earlier, Voce had bet Larwood "a pint of beer or a packet of fags" that he couldn't dislodge Singh's turban, which was duly sent in the direction of the slips. The terrors of Larwood and Voce would intensify just three weeks after the 10 for 10 game. When Nottinghamshire met Surrey at The Oval, the fast bowlers – along with Arthur Carr – would discuss strategy for the winter tour to Australia with the Surrey and England captain Douglas Jardine in the Grill Room of London's Piccadilly Hotel. Jardine would ask Larwood if he could bowl leg stump and make the ball "come up into the body" to compel Don Bradman to play his shots to leg. "Yes, I think that can be done," Larwood would reply, before spending the rest of the summer, along with Voce, trying "leg theory" on county batsmen.

In reality, types of Bodyline had been going on for years but were never fully channelled prior to Jardine. Voce had aimed in-swingers at the 1930 Australians at Trent Bridge, while Herbert Sutcliffe reckoned Yorkshire had faced fast leg-theory from Nottinghamshire for several seasons before 1932 – and proudly added that no one was allowed to back away. One man who never did that was Percy Holmes, who was renowned for his bravery against faster bowlers. Although closer to 50 years old than 40, Holmes withstood all Larwood could throw at him that Monday at Headingley with the fearlessness of someone half his age. Less than a fortnight earlier, Holmes had made what would be the last of his seven Test appearances against India at Lord's – India's first Test match and England's solitary Test of the 1932 season, for which Hedley Verity was not selected. After Holmes and Sutcliffe – plus Test debutant Bill Bowes – arrived in the capital in the early hours after a late finish to Yorkshire's match against Sussex at Leeds, the weary Holmes was bowled for six as England slid to 19 for three before recording a comfortable victory. Holmes would have played more for England but for the celebrated union of Sutcliffe and Jack Hobbs, which between 1924 and 1930 realised 15 century stands in 38 innings and 3,249 runs at 87. Although nearing the end of his career in 1932, and increasingly plagued by back and knee trouble, Holmes was still capable of class performances; in addition to his 224 not out in the 555 stand with Sutcliffe at Leyton, he'd scored 80s in the subsequent three Championship games before Nottinghamshire's visit.

According to the *Yorkshire Evening Post*, Larwood was bowling "ever so fast" on a pitch that had quickened due to the heat. Such was the speed of his sprint to the crease, Dick Moulton, the Headingley groundsman, had to remove tufts of turf scraped up by the bowler in his delivery stride. This caused a lengthy delay that disturbed the focus of Maurice Leyland, who was out soon after. Voce bowled him for five to leave Yorkshire in trouble at 37 for two. Leyland, who famously said that "none of us likes fast bowling, but some of us don't let on", was late on a ball that took middle stump and in the midst of a sterile season. The exception had been an innings of 189 against Middlesex at Sheffield a fortnight earlier, when he'd shared in a Yorkshire record second-wicket partnership of 346 with Wilf Barber, who made 162. It was Leyland's solitary century of the season but he'd bounce back with another four in August and the small matter of 1,013 runs in that month alone. It would inspire *Wisden* to declare that he "thoroughly rehabilitated his reputation as one of the leading batsmen of the day".

Leyland's wicket was just reward for Voce, who'd backed up Larwood from the Rugby Stand end. The pair were blood brothers on and off the field, and as junior partner in the frightening firm, Voce was subservient over choice of ends. Broad and big-muscled, with a 16-pace run-up, Voce was around six inches taller than Larwood but not as quick. However, he was still sharp enough to have sent Somerset batsman Cecil "Box" Case's bat flying out of his hands and on to the stumps earlier that year, the confused Case walking back to the pavilion clutching a stump instead of his bat. Voce had a whippy action and could dig the ball back into the ribs. It was his signature and the perfect foil for Larwood's straighter line. Like all great partnerships they worked together, helping generate wickets for each other. They also exerted psychological pressure over players who, if not physically bowled out, were often freaked out.

Popperfoto/Getty Images

Bill Voce – junior partner in Nottinghamshire's frightening pace bowling firm.

After Larwood and Voce's early incursions, Carr called on the brothers Staples, who were not so lethal in the lead-up to lunch. Holmes (60) and Barber (27) steadied the ship to steer Yorkshire into the break at 110 for two – just 124 behind – and well placed to forge a significant lead. Only once was Holmes's poise disturbed – ironically not by the bowlers but by the sound of workmen building the new stand. Fed-up with the constant clanging and crashing, which several times shattered his concentration, Holmes complained to umpire Harry Baldwin, who went behind the canvas screen to ask the foreman to keep down the noise. Holmes was normally a cheerful fellow; it was down to him that the Yorkshire side of the 1930s was known as "The Circus". Arriving late one night at the team hotel, the players found that a clerical error had left them without rooms. "The rooms are wanted for somebody and his circus," explained the hotel receptionist. "Well, they are wanted for Percy Holmes and his circus," the batsman insisted, and signed the register to that effect.

The morning sunshine had disappeared when the players returned for the afternoon session. Clouds had gathered in thundery skies and the heat had turned fiercely oppressive. The climactic change suited Larwood, who resumed the attack from the Kirkstall Lane end. He now found the weapon of cut through the air to transform the mood and complexion of the match. After Holmes added five to his lunchtime score, Larwood sent his middle stump "dancing fantastically". Holmes hit seven boundaries – four of them off Larwood – and was beaten for pace as he aimed towards leg. His dismissal, which left him on 999 runs for the season, ended a stand of 85 with Barber, who was reprieved on 34 in the same over. Larwood located the outside edge but Voce spilled a difficult chance at third slip.

The setback was temporary. After Brian Sellers was bowled for his third duck in five innings, playing too soon at Arthur Staples's slower ball and with a horizontal bat, Barber fell in Larwood's next over without adding to his score to leave Yorkshire 125 for five. Barber gave Larwood a hard-hit return but felt he'd been the victim of a bump ball. The orthodox Barber, whom Bill Bowes thought more of a textbook player than Len Hutton, and who never considered his own efforts worthy, received a sympathetic hand as he left the field. Barely had the ovation subsided when loud cheers rang out for Arthur Mitchell, who unexpectedly resumed his innings against the man who'd forced him to retire hurt. Larwood surveyed his quarry with gimlet eye and predictably greeted Mitchell with another short ball. Equally predictably, it struck Mitchell's bad hand, drawing oohs and aahs from the crowd and a cold grin from Larwood, for whom Mitchell's return was a red rag to a bull. After removing his glove and wringing his hand, Mitchell indicated he was fit to continue, drawing further cheers. Thereafter, he seemed to wince every time the ball hit his bat.

Ron Deaton collection

"As grim as a piece of stone from Baildon Moor" – the uncompromising Arthur Mitchell, who was cheered to the echo when he bravely resumed his innings after being hit by Harold Larwood.

Mitchell's toughness was legendary. Not only did he symbolise Yorkshire grit, the ability to withstand hurdles and hardship, he was as harsh and hard-nosed as they come. Mitchell despised frippery or frivolity of any description, considering it weakness. When his Yorkshire team-mate Ellis Robinson took a brilliant diving catch, the acclaim of the crowd ringing in his ears, Mitchell barked: "Gerrup, tha's makkin an exhibition o'thisen." Len Hutton described Mitchell as "too hard for me", while Herbert Sutcliffe said he was "as grim as a piece of stone from Baildon Moor". Mitchell had added three to his earlier 11 when the skies darkened further and rain forced the teams off with Yorkshire 128 for five. The delay lasted 20 minutes, the sixth wicket falling in the first over after the restart when Larwood

Getty Images

Verity batting against Sussex at Hove one month after the 10 for 10 match. Yorkshire beat Sussex by 167 runs to clinch the Championship.

bowled Arthur Wood for one. When Voce had Arthur Rhodes caught at short-leg off another short ball, Yorkshire had lost five for 13 and the total was 135 for seven. Into this cauldron of concern walked Hedley Verity.

Verity was a competent batsman who could normally be relied on to hold up an end. R. C. Robertson-Glasgow said "a casual observer might have mistaken Verity for Sutcliffe a little out of form, for he seemed to have caught something of that master's style and gesture". Robertson-Glasgow added that both men could be "clean bowled in a manner that somehow exonerated the batsman from all guilt". Like Wilfred Rhodes, Verity would open the batting for England, and he'd finish with a first-class average of 18 and a top score of 101 for Yorkshire against Jamaica at Sabina Park in 1936. In Larwood, Verity faced an opponent for whom he had the utmost regard. Verity felt it would be "well-nigh impossible" to improve on Larwood's action and admired the "easy yet straight and fast run" and the way, as he entered his delivery stride, Larwood "seemed to be trying to grow taller before arm and body swept through, putting his last ounce behind the delivery to complete a beautiful effort". Verity should have fallen to Larwood when he had four and the total was 140 but wicket-keeper Ben Lilley – hampered by a strained tendon in his right instep suffered while batting – dropped him, the catch so straightforward that umpire Bill Reeves raised his finger only to retract it when the ball went to ground. Lilley regarded injuries as an occupational hazard; at the end of each season, he'd say his fingers ached so much from keeping to Larwood that he had to boil them in water to loosen the joints.

Verity scrapped and scraped his way to 12 before Larwood beat him with a ball that sent one of the bails flying "quite 15 yards". *The Times* said "Verity's stroke suggested he had lost sight of the ball altogether". Verity was Larwood's fifth victim and his dismissal left Yorkshire 152 for eight. It was Larwood's sixth five-wicket haul in eight innings – the high-water mark of a season that would be his best in wicket-taking terms. Mitchell's brave resistance ended when he was run out for 24 by partner George Macaulay, who played Larwood in the direction of mid-off and called for a single in his apparent anxiety to get off strike. Spotting the swooping Willis Walker, Macaulay stopped, changed his mind and sent back Mitchell, who was beaten by a direct hit. Macaulay edged two lucky fours off Larwood – and last man Bill Bowes scratched a single – before bad light stopped play at 3.50 p.m., closely followed by rain so heavy it prevented a restart. Yorkshire were 163 for nine and Larwood had five for 73 from 22 overs, the *Nottingham Evening News* insisting he had "never bowled better" and "evidently he means to go to Australia".

As Larwood rested in the pavilion, and as Yorkshire contemplated a deficit of 71, the outfield soon became submerged. What began as a day so beautiful that the *Yorkshire Evening News* said "women spectators wore the flimsiest of clothing and many of the men discarded their jackets and collars" now saw those same spectators inappropriately attired for the worsening weather. "Hats and frocks suffered grievously when the rain came," reported *Leeds Mercury* columnist Frank North. "The most striking male fashion was that displayed by a young man near the scoreboard. I wondered whether he represented a hiker or a lifeboat man. When the storm broke, the answer was easy." North added: "Cricket is a great game. It develops patience, determination and hardihood. That was obvious at Headingley. Hundreds of spectators refused to leave the ground after play stopped. Two hours later many were still there. The fact that spectators are willing to suffer thunder, lightning and drenching rain in order to see a few more overs bowled proves my contention that cricket is a great little game. For the rest, a little excitement was caused by a commissionaire chasing a youth halfway round the ground. The youth, it appears, had attempted to see the game without going through the formality of the turnstiles."

The storm to which North referred was no ordinary downpour. Later that night, in the Broad Acres and beyond, the weather broke spectacularly after the weekend heatwave. In Leeds city centre, about a mile from the ground, an inch of rain fell in just over four hours and hailstones were sighted an inch in diameter. In Bradford, a labourer named Manfred Clough was killed by lightning, his clothing scorched and a boot torn off. Torrential rain fell in Dewsbury, where the local cinema was struck by lightning, causing plaster to fall on the audience and badly injuring a Rueben Ramsden, who was detained overnight in the local infirmary. Thousands of turnips were washed away in Pickering, while people on the outskirts of Leeds saw cows and goats swimming past a gasworks, the animals carried by the raging torrents. Among the worst hit areas was Barnoldswick, North Yorkshire, where the Ouzedale Foundry was all but destroyed. "Barnoldswick is a place of devastation," reported the *Yorkshire Evening News*. "The majority of the town's 4,000 cotton workers are out of work, and owners of a number of small businesses are to be seen sorting out the wreckage of their shop interiors." Further afield, five inches of rain fell in less than three hours in Cranwell, Lincolnshire, extensive flooding was reported in Nottinghamshire, while lightning struck the roof of Leicester Stadium, hurling slates and tiles over 100 yards. The fuse box responsible for powering the stadium's electric hare was burnt out – and the hare itself engulfed in flames.

It was all in dramatic contrast to the previous few days, when Britain had basked in scorching temperatures. In Croydon, a heat mist laden with millions of greenfly had been sighted near a local aerodrome, forcing cyclists to dismount and producing an effect resembling green-tinted smoke moving in the breeze. At London's Fortune Theatre, Colonel F. A. Wilson, a member of the British College of Psychic Science, collapsed and died on stage due to the heat, his last words "truth will conquer in the end". So boiling had it been in Blackpool that a young woman on the town's Central Beach was forced to abandon a sponsored fast, the *Yorkshire Post* reporting:

> *Mrs Nellie Hayes, the 22-year-old Blackpool shop girl, who entered a barrel in an attempt to fast ten days and ten nights, has given up the attempt. She had been in the barrel 33 hours without food or water, but the reason she gave up was because of the excessive heat. As she left the barrel, Mrs Lily Jones, of Cardiff, aged 22, stepped into it to make a similar effort. She was shaded from the heat by a large umbrella.*

Elsewhere on Monday 11 July, only 10 minutes' play was possible at the Bath Festival, where Somerset advanced from 141 for three to 152 for three in reply to Glamorgan's 110. There was no play after 2.50 at Blackheath, where Les Ames's third successive century took Kent from 78 for one to 269 for six in response to Surrey's 345. The final session was washed out at Northampton, where Wally Hammond (92) and Ces Dacre (76) lifted Gloucestershire to 245 for three and a lead of

368. And at Coventry, where Warwickshire were 58 for nought in their second innings, a lead of 118 against Leicestershire, there was no play after 3.30. There were interruptions too at Chesterfield, where Essex were 192 for eight after Derbyshire's 487 for nine declared, and at Southampton, where Hampshire were 51 for two in their second innings against Middlesex, 153 behind. Perversely, the only game not affected was in typically wet Manchester, where the Indians were 157 for four following-on – 81 adrift. As for the sides at Headingley, the most significant action came at Kidderminster, where Sussex swept to a two-day win over Worcestershire to climb above Nottinghamshire into third place. Only one run separated Sussex and Worcestershire on first innings, but after the hosts were dismissed for 111 second time round, Ted Bowley and captain Duleepsinhji steered the visitors to a nine-wicket triumph.

Sussex's victory meant Nottinghamshire had to gain at least a draw at Leeds to reclaim third position. After their ponderous performance on the opening day, Carr's men had fought back magnificently to seize the match by the scruff of the neck. However, their victory hopes now appeared dependent on the weather. Apart from a brief hiatus on Monday afternoon, when the covers were fleetingly removed in the hope of a 6.15 restart, it rained solidly in Headingley from 4.00 until midnight. Nor was Tuesday's forecast promising. There were predictions of further showers and possibly longer periods of rain. For Hedley Verity and his Yorkshire team-mates, it seemed the elements might ride to their rescue. As the *Yorkshire Post* put it, "It will be hard luck for Notts if the rain continues to prevent any more play in this match in which the bowling of Larwood and Voce has given them such a big advantage."

6

An Avalanche from Heaven

Given anything like strong sunshine it is just possible that some startling and dramatic cricket may be seen at Headingley. Rain fell in such quantities last night as to completely soak the wicket and, at twenty minutes to six, the proceedings were abandoned.

So proclaimed the *Nottingham Guardian* on the final morning of the 10 for 10 game. It would be even more prescient than the paper envisaged as Hedley Verity made cricketing history. The writer saw not the potential of a Yorkshire victory but the prospect of a famous Nottinghamshire win. If the visitors showed dash in their second innings – equipped with a handy first innings lead – they could declare and get Yorkshire in trouble on a sticky wicket if the sun dried the pitch.

That pitch had recovered remarkably well by the time the teams arrived at the ground. Although too damp for an 11.30 start, play was deemed possible from 12.30 in conditions that remained grey and gloomy. Only a few hundred had braved the weather, with the crowd also down at the Great Yorkshire Show, just 4,639 turning out at nearby Temple Newsam compared to 10,821 the previous year. Entries at the show comprised 569 pigeons, 157 pigs, 103 goats and 38 dairy cows including a British Friesian named Chaddesley Hedge Rose II, dubbed "The Wonder Cow" after five successes at the Royal Show.

Shortly before 12.30, the Yorkshire captain Brian Sellers went out to inspect the wicket with his team-mates Percy Holmes, Herbert Sutcliffe, Maurice Leyland and Arthur Wood. The quintet studied the surface closely, as though reading a map of buried treasure, and discussed their findings among themselves. Although Sellers was autocratic, he was never too proud to ask for advice and, before the toss, would often seek the views of Holmes and Sutcliffe followed by those of Verity and Bowes. Whenever Yorkshire won the toss, Bowes admitted he never knew whether Sellers had taken his and Verity's counsel or that of the batsmen. The consequence of this discussion was that Sellers declared Yorkshire's first innings closed at the overnight 163 for nine, thereby conceding a lead of 71 and first innings points to Nottinghamshire. In those days, sides gained five points for a first innings lead in a drawn game, three points if they had the lower first innings score in a drawn game, or 15 points for a win. Sellers thus sacrificed first innings points if the match finished drawn in an effort to win the contest outright. It was a clear challenge to Nottinghamshire captain Arthur Carr to set Yorkshire a target despite the danger of the hosts being ambushed.

Some newspapers hailed Sellers's tactic an audacious gamble, one correspondent calling it a move that "fair took the breath away". Although it showed his aggression and ambition to win, it was, in reality, no daring speculation. There was little hope of the innings lasting much longer, or of Yorkshire achieving first innings points. With just one wicket left and the hapless Bowes a shooting target, Sellers was actually risking little – particularly as some observers felt the overhead conditions might assist his quicker bowlers. However, the threadbare crowd applauded Sellers when

Yorkshire took to the field with a new face on board – that of twelfth man Frank Dennis, deputising for the injured Arthur Mitchell, who watched from the pavilion with his damaged hand bandaged. Dennis, 25, a fast-medium bowler from Leeds and future brother-in-law of Len Hutton, was physically striking with a six-foot frame and barrel chest. He first played for Yorkshire in 1928 but only occasionally after 1930. In 1948, he'd emigrate to New Zealand to take up fruit farming before becoming a selector for the Canterbury Cricket Association.

As work on the Rugby Stand continued, with the cacophony of cement mixers providing an unholy soundtrack to this blessed sporting day, Bowes began the innings with a no-ball to Walter Keeton from the Kirkstall Lane end. The third ball of the over was short and Keeton, on to it in a flash, hooked it for four, defeating Holmes's attempt to stop it on the boundary. The fifth ball was another half-tracker and Keeton this time hooked it for three, Holmes preventing another boundary with a fine diving stop. Yet that rush of runs was no barometer of intent as, much to Sellers's frustration, Nottinghamshire declined his challenge to set up a game, their second innings settling into the soporific and plodding pattern of the first. The wicket, which was slow and low, encouraged neither strokemaking nor wicket-taking and Bowes battled in vain for an early breakthrough. "The fast bowler could get nothing out of the pitch," reported the *Yorkshire Post*. "The ball did not move as had been thought likely." George Macaulay, who opened from the Rugby Stand end, could get little out of it either and Nottinghamshire – on Carr's command – betrayed contentment with first innings points as they doggedly set to bat out the draw. Amid the sequence of dead-bats and dot-balls, Shipston momentarily relieved the monotony, late-cutting Macaulay for four to the junction of the Western Terrace and Kirkstall Lane end. Shipston was enjoying his most prolific season, one that would bring 461 runs at 35.46, including hundreds against Hampshire and Glamorgan, but here he was cautious beneath cloudy skies. Keeton, whom R. C. Robertson-Glasgow called "strung-up, concentrated, quick-glancing", was similarly watchful. In the corresponding fixture the following year, which Yorkshire would win by 10 wickets at Bradford, Keeton would hit a hundred before lunch and Verity would not take a wicket in the innings.

When the total at Headingley was 23, Sellers turned to his left-arm spinner, who replaced Macaulay at the Rugby Stand end. Macaulay followed Bowes at the Kirkstall Lane side and the cricket laboured in the lead-up to lunch. Verity's seven overs prior to the break were maidens and although both he and Macaulay made the ball turn, they did not do so quickly enough to trouble the batsmen. Both Keeton and Shipston had 18 when Nottinghamshire dined on 38 for nought after an hour's cricket of forgettable character. According to the *Yorkshire Post*, "Verity had asked to be hit at least twice every over" and "never looked like taking a wicket". The paper added that each batsman had scored "almost as many runs as he had failed to get", so ultra-defensive were Nottinghamshire's tactics. The *Yorkshire Evening Post* said "the batsmen just contented themselves with letting the ball hit the bat", while the *Nottingham Evening Post* remarked that "it was difficult to understand the attitude of the Notts' batsmen". As the *Yorkshire Post* observed: "The spectators had had the Notts' caution impressed upon them and they were prepared for a wearying afternoon."

Among the crowd was Verity's father, who watched with a group of friends from Rawdon. Instinctively weighing the atmosphere and conditions, he told them: "You need not bother at all until Hedley brings up his second slip; then you can sit up and take notice." Suddenly, one ball spun significantly after lunch and Holmes was summoned to reinforce the cordon. Hazy sunshine began to break through and the drying surface started to bite. Verity's first two overs after the interval were also maidens, giving him figures at that stage of 9-9-0-0. From the third ball of his 10th over, Shipston scored a lucky two, edging streakily over the slips. Verity's next over was another maiden and he captured the first of his 10 wickets with the opening ball of his 12th over. Keeton, on 21, pushed forward and was caught at first slip by Macaulay, the ball turning quickly from an off stump line as Nottinghamshire slipped to 44 for one.

Verity's pace was normally slow medium; on quicker pitches this rose to medium. He'd bowl faster whenever the pitch was turning and flight it more on a batsman's wicket. On stickier surfaces like that at Leeds, he'd increase his speed and try to make the batsmen play. "Such is sticky wicket bowling par excellence," he'd say, "the method adopted by all great spin bowlers when attacking with conditions in their favour." At all times, regardless of conditions, Verity focused on finding good length. He called this "the secret of good bowling" and defined it as "the shortest length at which a batsman should play forward". This, said Verity, was "the ABC of bowling". He further believed the ideal left-arm spinner's ball "pitches on a good length and turns quickly away to the off", adding that "if it can be pitched on the leg and middle so much the better for then even the Bradmans and Sutcliffes are in trouble".

With the sun-drying surface supplying more zip, batting was harder than it was before lunch, but the pitch was by no means a hazardous gluepot. In Verity's next over, Willis Walker was twice fortunate not to be bowled before stealing a single off the fifth delivery. Shipston fell at the start of Verity's 14th over, caught by wicketkeeper Wood for 21 as Nottinghamshire dropped to 47 for two (the Nottinghamshire scorebook gives the wicket to the first ball of the over and the Yorkshire scorebook to the second ball). Shipston also got a delivery that turned quickly from around off stump but a faster one than did for Keeton, the sort of variation Bowes observed could "knock the stumps flying". Bowes said Verity used this quicker ball "about 16 times a season and it gave him 16 wickets".

Shipston's departure, after a painstaking 90-minute vigil, brought Carr to the crease on a pair. He duly "bagged it" as Verity got him with the first delivery of his 15th over, Nottinghamshire sliding to 51 for three. As in the first innings, Carr tried to hit a six towards the new stand and was caught by Wilf Barber in front of the sightscreen. The *Yorkshire Evening Post* said Barber "had not to run as far as he had when he caught Carr in the first innings", while Herbert Sutcliffe reckoned Carr was twice unlucky, writing that "each shot was just about worth the six it would have got had the ball travelled another two or three yards".

Carr, whose aggression contradicted his safety-first orders, also attributed his failures to misfortune. He felt they'd been caused by his green batting gloves, which he'd never before worn in a first-class match. "Like a fool", Carr had bought the gloves two years earlier despite thinking green things brought him bad luck. This superstition began in 1926 when, to celebrate being made England captain, he'd bought a green car that gave nothing but grief. Driving the car in his green club tie, Carr crashed into a lorry en route to Trent Bridge. Later that year, following a game against Surrey, he drove team-mates "Dodge" Whysall, Sam Staples and Fred Barratt to Hastings and collided with a telegraph pole, Barratt sustaining serious cuts. When Carr sold the vehicle a short time later, his luck changed immediately. His mother won a race at Newbury with *Honey Maker*, and his father the Newbury Cup with *Try Try Again*, the loyal son banking handsome winnings. Carr, in fact, was routinely involved in motoring mishaps. These were normally the product of excess alcohol – and nothing to do with the colour green. Once, Carr was so desperate to take delivery of a crate of beer, he tried to drive his car into a pub, reluctantly abandoning the plan when it failed to fit through the double doors. Another time, he was driving two team-mates at breakneck speed when one fell out after falling asleep, with neither Carr nor the other man noticing. A policeman appeared and, by way of a sobriety test, asked him to say: "Sister Susie's sewing shirts for soldiers." Carr protested: "Damn it, I can't say that when I'm stone cold sober." The policeman let him go.

After Verity got him for the second time at Leeds, Carr hurled his gloves on the dressing room floor. These were the gloves Frank Shipston remembered landed at his feet. Bill Bowes wrote: "To say he [Carr] was annoyed is an understatement. He went back to his dressing room, collected his bag and all his equipment and threw them into the

Nottinghamshire captain Arthur Carr, who threw away his green batting gloves in a fit of fury after Verity dismissed him for the second time at Leeds.

professionals' room. 'Here, take the lot,' he said. 'It's a hell of a lot of good to me when I get a pair.'" It was the second time that year he'd chucked away his stuff. The first time, recognising he might have been a touch hasty, Carr swallowed his pride. He returned to the dressing room and asked for it back. "This time," said Bowes, "he didn't get the chance … it went irretrievably." Harold Larwood took pity on his captain. He lent him one of his bats and promised he could keep it if he made a fifty in the next match. Carr did twice as well – he made a century – and the bat became one of his favourites. Carr's failures against Verity finally convinced him to turn his back on green things. "The combination of green and ill-luck has so impressed me that I never like the colour and will not have anything to do with green things if I can help it," he declared.

Another with cause to rue his misfortune at Headingley was Macaulay, who bowled magnificently after lunch as Carr's men struggled on the drying deck. According to the *Yorkshire Evening Post*, Macaulay had "the hardest of luck", many times going past the bat but spinning the ball with such revolution his opponents weren't good enough to get the edge. Verity spun it just enough and, allied to his ability to make the ball lift, a skill intensified in wet conditions and a weapon known as his "perching ball", he thrived in contrast to his thwarted team-mate. Verity's facility for finding the edge was fondly remembered by Ellis Robinson, an off-spinner who represented Yorkshire from 1934 to 1949. Robinson referred to Verity as "Clear Gum", his nickname in the Yorkshire dressing room because, towards the end of his career, Verity advertised *Rowntrees Clear Gums* – "the nation's favourite sweet", as the slogan said. In his South Yorkshire brogue, Robinson would reflect: "Clear Gum 'tonned' it just enough – half a bat. I used to 'ton' it too much – that's why t'ball kept slipping down t'leg side." Verity shared out the gums with his team-mates and took any left-overs back to his family.

While Macaulay huffed and puffed in the Headingley sunshine, Verity continued to blow the house down. After his 16th over was a maiden and the 17th his most expensive, with Arthur Staples hitting the first delivery – a rank full toss – for three to leg, and Walker taking a single off the fourth ball, Verity spectacularly changed the course of the match. With the total at 63 for three, a seemingly impregnable lead of 134, he took a hat-trick with the second, third and fourth deliveries of his 18th over, a triple-wicket maiden. First, Walker was brilliantly caught at first slip by Macaulay, who shot out his right hand to somehow grab a ball that was going away from him. Walker had been trying to drive down the ground after making patchy progress to 11. Macaulay was a splendid slip but did not always field there due to the presence of Arthur Mitchell. Once, in a match at Old Trafford, Macaulay took two magnificent slip catches off

Bowes, who teased him with the words: "I don't mind telling you, Mac, that every time I see a catch going to you my heart comes into my mouth." "Well," replied Macaulay, "there's plenty of room for it – what are you grumbling about?" Verity drew another close catch when Charlie Harris, prodding forward, edged to Holmes at second slip, the veteran pouching another sharp chance. It brought in George Vernon Gunn for the hat-trick ball.

Verity had never had a hat-trick for Yorkshire. The last Yorkshire player to take one had been his old tutor, Emmott Robinson, against Kent at Gravesend in 1930. Now Verity cleverly outwitted his opponent; with the close field set deeper, as though flagging the prospect of a quicker delivery, Gunn was already back on his heels to a looping straight ball and plumb lbw when he should have played forward. In an eye-blink, Nottinghamshire had nosedived to 63 for six – effectively 134 for six – and the day had dramatically come alive. "The crowd roared with delight," reported the *Yorkshire Evening News*. "Needless to say, there were no slumbering spectators now."

Verity was on an unstoppable roll; it was clear in his stride and sprightly demeanour. No sooner had he bowled than he craved the ball back; when it was thrown to him by the fielders and wicketkeeper, he snatched at it busily, impatient to feel it in the palm of his hand. This complete immersion was typical of Verity. On the rare occasions he was not absorbed, it was said that all you had to do to get him going was to tell him that everything depended on him, while at the same time expressing doubt in his powers. Verity's focus was etched on his face, R. C. Robertson-Glasgow once noting how he "peered down the pitch after each ball, suggesting a chemist watching the perilous crucible, the connoisseur nosing the dubious vase, or even a conjurer investing simplicity with mystery". J. M. Kilburn said "Verity's menace you can see and share from the spectator's seat", adding that "Verity upon a day of success is the personification of hostility". Kilburn felt "you can appreciate the fact that the ball leaves his hand with some imp of evil in it; Verity himself announces it as he stoops forward at the end of his follow-through or throws up an expectant arm as the batsman plunges blindly to the approximate pitch".

Following Verity's hat-trick at Headingley, not only was a Yorkshire win a possibility, but also the chance he could single-handedly run through the visitors. "In the midst of the sensations the question was whether Verity would succeed in claiming all ten wickets," observed the *Nottingham Evening News*, "and while we were still talking about it Verity, at 64, took two more wickets with successive deliveries." From the penultimate ball of his 19th over, Verity had Arthur Staples caught at first slip by Macaulay for seven before Harold Larwood – trying to hit straight – sliced into the offside and was brilliantly held by Sutcliffe running back from cover point; "a gem of a catch", purred the *Leeds Mercury*. Verity, at that stage, had eight for seven – the only time in the innings when his wickets exceeded his runs conceded. "The enthusiasm of the crowd knew no bounds," said the *Nottingham Evening News*, and yet there was little time for spectators to appreciate what they were witnessing. Although a 10-wicket haul had become increasingly likely, such feats were not then uncommon and the prospect of a world record being broken was unlikely to have crossed their minds amid the speed of the collapse. The greatest bowling figures in first-class cricket at the time were 10 for 18, recorded three years earlier by Leicestershire

pace bowler George Geary on a treacherous pitch against
Glamorgan at Pontypridd. Quite how many at Headingley
would have known that, however, or had it in mind even if
they did – let alone realised Verity's figures – is debatable.
Record-keeping was not as comprehensive as it is today
(there was no *Cricinfo* or *Cricket Archive* to provide statistical reference), while there was only one scoreboard at
Headingley and it was a primitive affair that did not give
out bowling figures. The scoreboard was situated at the
Kirkstall Lane end, roughly where the Trueman Enclosure
is today. It contained only basic information such as the
team total and number of wickets fallen, the scores of the
two batsmen, the total of the last man and fall of the last

Ted Kirwan

wicket. Unlike the giant
scoreboards on Australian
Test grounds, it listed
neither bowlers' wickets nor
runs conceded. Whenever a
batsman is nearing a major
milestone, such as when
Don Bradman made succes-
sive triple hundreds at Leeds
in the 1930s, the first of
which broke the world Test
record, his score is clear and
there is time for drama to
develop and records to be
checked. Verity's perfor-
mance was over in a flash.
Faster, almost, than you
could say "Sister Susie's
sewing shirts for soldiers".

*Leicestershire pace bowler George
Geary, the previous holder of the
record figures in first-class cricket.*

After dismissing Staples and Larwood, Verity was on another hat-trick at the start of his 20th over. Only once in the game's history had a player taken two hat-tricks in the same innings – Albert Trott claiming four wickets in four balls, followed by three in three, during his benefit match for Middlesex against Somerset at Lord's in 1907. One of the best all-rounders of the Golden Age, Trott was a powerful batsman and round-arm bowler who played for his native Australia and later England before committing suicide in 1914, aged 41. Suffering from dropsy, and living alone and penniless in London digs, he wrote his will on the back of a laundry ticket before shooting himself.

Trott's record survived – just. To gasps from the crowd, which dissolved into groans, Ben Lilley thrust out a hopeful bat at the hat-trick ball, which took the inside edge and missed leg stump by a whisker, running away for three to fine-leg. Bill Voce kept out the second delivery of the over but edged the third to Holmes at second slip to depart for a duck. It left Nottinghamshire nine down and brought to the crease last man Sam Staples. As a 2,000 crowd looked on spellbound, Verity's first ball to the No. 11 was devilishly flighted, Staples over-balanced in an effort to reach it and Wood broke the stumps with a showman's flourish. Nottinghamshire were all out for 67 and Verity, incredibly, had 10 for 10. "There were scenes of great enthusiasm when Verity got Sam Staples stumped and completed the string of ten wickets," said the *Nottingham Guardian*, "and every player on the Yorkshire side rushed to congratulate him." The *Nottingham Evening News* referenced "scenes of wild excitement when the last wicket fell", while the *Yorkshire Post* said "the crowd rushed from the terraces to applaud his wonderful work".

After his 10 for 36 against Warwickshire in 1931, Verity had called his 16th over – in which he'd taken four wickets – "an avalanche from heaven". It was a sweet turn of phrase but more suited to this follow-up. Having taken three for seven with his first 103 balls, Verity claimed seven for three with his final 15. Of the 118 deliveries he sent down in total, a staggering 113 were not scored off. Verity was only the third man after "Tich" Freeman and Middlesex slow underarm bowler Vyell Walker to take 10 wickets in an innings more than once. His was the 45th 10-wicket haul in first-class cricket and, as against Warwickshire, eight of his victims were caught, one lbw and one stumped. Nottinghamshire's innings lasted 130 minutes and the wickets fell in a 60-minute spell after lunch. One minute, the visitors had been batting to a dreary draw; the next, they were crushed beneath the wheels of a juggernaut they simply couldn't stop and never saw coming.

VERITY'S WICKET-TO-WICKET ANALYSIS

WICKET	BATSMAN OUT	VERITY'S FIGURES
1	KEETON	11.1-10-2-1
*2	SHIPSTON	13.1/13.2-11-3-2
3	CARR	14.1-12-3-3
4	WALKER	17.2-14-7-4
5	HARRIS	17.3-14-7-5
6	GUNN	17.4-14-7-6
7	A. STAPLES	18.5-15-7-7
8	LARWOOD	18.6-15-7-8
9	VOCE	19.3-16-10-9
10	S. STAPLES	19.4-16-10-10

*The Yorkshire and Nottinghamshire scorebooks disagree as to which ball of the over the second wicket fell.

Carr led a chastened team on to the field when Yorkshire began their second innings at 3.40 p.m., needing 139 to win. There were 50 minutes left until tea and a maximum of two-and-a-half hours available for play in weather that had returned overcast. Carr threw the ball to Larwood, whose second delivery Percy Holmes dropped into the leg-side for a single that completed his 1,000 runs for the season. Larwood struggled to get much out of the pitch, so Carr took him off after only three overs, rotating Voce and Arthur Staples at the Kirkstall Lane side and using Sam Staples's off-spin from the end exploited so sensationally by Verity.

Whereas Verity had been irresistible, Staples was innocuous. Unable to reprise his match-winning performance in the corresponding game in 1923, he was milked by the masterly Holmes and Sutcliffe, who'd shaved 81 runs off the target by tea (Holmes 43, Sutcliffe 30). Throughout their association, the partners were known as "Holmes and Sutcliffe" – as opposed to the other way round – despite the fact Holmes was second fiddle to his colleague's first violin. Their friendship had begun before the Great War, when they'd met on the top tier of a Leeds tramcar after spotting each other's cricket bags. They first opened in 1919 and formed cricket's most prolific opening partnership, sharing 69 century stands for Yorkshire and 74 overall. This was number 72 and, considering what preceded it, the most astonishing.

Holmes went to fifty after tea and, thought the *Leeds Mercury*, had "rarely played more confidently". Sutcliffe was self-assured too but did have a life on 39 when Charlie Harris dropped him at cover off Voce. The scoring rate was swift but conditions remained challenging. The difference was that Nottinghamshire did not have anyone to maximise them as Verity had done. Although Holmes and Sutcliffe were sometimes beaten, they remained in control. "Odd balls 'popped'," said the *Yorkshire Post*, "and always they turned, but Yorkshire's batting was immaculate." Sutcliffe's ability to scrub from his mind any minor success enjoyed by a bowler was legendary. Don Bradman reckoned he had the best temperament of anyone he played against, while Neville Cardus wrote that "if a ball should beat him he appeared to be interested rather than worried".

At 5.40 p.m., it was all over, Holmes striking the winning runs off Sam Staples to finish unbeaten on 77, Sutcliffe undefeated on 54. Sam Staples bowled 18.4 overs (exactly one less than Verity) and took nought for 37. As the *Yorkshire Post* observed, "They [Holmes and Sutcliffe] had made the Notts' bowling look as ineffective as the Notts' batting." According to the *Nottingham Evening News*, the visitors' defeat could not be blamed on the pitch. "Had it not been for the superlative batting of the Yorkshire 'twins', Notts' third defeat of the season might have been softened by the story of a difficult pitch, but as Holmes and Sutcliffe scored their 100 runs in little more than an hour, despite repeated changes of bowling, excuses would be futile … Flight was the secret of Verity's bowling successes, but at the height of the collapse I think Notts were spelling it with an 'r' in place of the 'l'." *The Times* noted that the pitch gave the bowlers "some assistance" but said "while Verity could not have accomplished his outstanding success without its aid, it was only an accessory after his flight and length, which continually made the batsmen play the strokes they did not wish to after the ball had pitched". The *Yorkshire Evening Post* insisted: "There was nothing in the state of the wicket to account for the phenomenal fall of Notts; it would be to deprive Verity of the full credit of his performance to suggest there was."

YORKSHIRE v. NOTTINGHAMSHIRE, at Headingley
Sat., Mon., and Tues., July 9th, 11th, and 12th, 1932.

NOTTINGHAMSHIRE.

	1st Innings		2nd Innings	
1. Keeton b Rhodes	...		c Macaulay b Verity	21
2. Shipstone b Macaulay	8		b Wood b Verity	
3. Walker c Barber b Bowes	36		c Macaulay b Verity	11
4. A. W. Carr c Barber b Verity	3		c Barber b Verity	
5. Staples (A.) b Macaulay			c Macaulay b Verity	
6. Harris lbw b Leyland	35		c Holmes b Verity	
7. Gunn (G. V.) b Verity	31		not out	
8. Lilley not out	46		lbw b Verity	
9. Voce b Leyland			c Holmes b Verity	
10. Larwood	0		c Holmes b Verity	
11. Staples (S.) b Leyland			st Wood b Verity	
Extras b 8, lb 6, w 2, nb 2	18		Extras b 3, nb 1	4
Total	234		Total	67

Total runs at fall of each wicket
15 35 40 46 67 120 199 233 234 | 1 44 47 51 53 63 63 64 64 67 67

Bowler	Overs	Maidens	Runs	W'kts	Overs	Maidens	Runs	W'kts
Bowes	31	9	85	1	5	0	19	0
Rhodes	28	13	49	0				
Verity	41	18	64	2	19.4	16	10	10
Macaulay	8.2	3	24	1	23	9	34	0
Leyland	3	1	4	3				

Umpires: Messrs. Baldwin & Reeves.   Scorers: Messrs. Ringrose & Carlin.

YORKSHIRE.

	1st Innings		2nd Innings	
1. Holmes b Larwood	65		not out	77
2. Sutcliffe c Voce b Larwood	not out		not out	54
3. Mitchell run out				
4. Leyland b Voce	24			
5. Barber c and b Larwood	34			
6. A. B. Sellers b Staples (A.)				
7. Wood b Larwood				
8. Rhodes c Staples (A.) b Voce				
9. Verity b Staples				
10. Macaulay not out				
11. Bowes not out				
Extras b 5, lb 5	10		Extras b 4, lb 4	8
Total for 9 wkts, dec.	163		Total for 0 wkt.	139

Total runs at fall of each wicket
1 37 121 123 125 128 135 152 154 | —

Bowler	Overs	Maidens	Runs	W'kts	Overs	Maidens	Runs	W'kts
Larwood	32	4	73	5	14	0	43	0
Voce	22	2	52	2	10	0	37	0
Staples (S.)	7	3	20	1	18.4	6	25	0
Staples (A.)	11		3		6	0	12	0
Harris					3	0	8	0

Hours of Play—1st & 2nd Days, 11.30 to 6.30; 3rd Day, 11.30 to 6.0. Tea, 4.15.
Luncheon interval, 1.30 to 2.10 each day.

H. Verity

The historic scorecard signed by Verity. (William H. Roberts)

Yorkshire's ninth victory of the season sent them top of the table with 160 points from 17 games, two points ahead of Kent, who managed only three points as their match against Surrey at Blackheath was drawn. Sussex were third on 128 after their win over Worcestershire, Nottinghamshire fourth on 127. At the Bath Festival, where Somerset thrashed Glamorgan by an innings and 31 runs, Jack White almost emulated Verity's feat of taking 10 wickets, returning nine for 51 – and catching the other batsman. Elsewhere, Gloucestershire thumped Northamptonshire by 262 runs, Derbyshire trounced Essex by an innings and 171 runs, Middlesex beat Hampshire by nine wickets and Lancashire defeated the Indians by six wickets, rain consigning Warwickshire's game against Leicestershire to a draw.

At Headingley, where the forecast rain never materialised, Carr was the first to congratulate Verity. "It is a great performance," he told him, "but I wish you had done it on somebody else instead of Nottingham." Verity signed spectators' scorecards before saying the rest must wait for another time. Before returning home, he posed for a photograph outside the ground in the only record of his red-letter day. Dapper and debonair in his Yorkshire blazer, with the white rose emblem above the left pocket, he is pictured shaking hands with Bright Heyhirst, the Yorkshire masseur, a small, avuncular figure wearing spectacles and a smile. Verity, his face turned towards Heyhirst, is smiling too but looks stiff and awkward, as though he can't wait for the fuss to be over. To his left is Arthur Mitchell, the lower half of his left hand tucked into his trouser pocket and his bandaged right hand hidden from view, and to his left is Frank Dennis, who strikes a near identical pose. Also in the photograph is Arthur Wood, caught in profile on the far left of shot, and

Verity family collection

Verity is congratulated on his 10 for 10 by Yorkshire masseur Bright Heyhirst as, from left, Arthur Wood, George Macaulay, Arthur Mitchell and Frank Dennis share his triumph.

George Macaulay, who stands between Wood and Heyhirst and smiles directly at the camera, his fingers pressed into his blazer pockets and his thumbs poking out of them, as though there wasn't sufficient room for them too.

History does not record how Verity celebrated his 10 for 10. Len Hutton said he was "never a man for the taproom", pointing out that Verity "liked a drink – a glass of wine or a pint of beer at the close of play – but he was really a temperate man". Hutton added: "He was fond of a pipe. But he didn't smoke heavily, perhaps just the odd cigarette at the tea interval or after the match." According to Douglas Verity, the Verity family have never been drinkers. "When grandfather won a bottle of sherry in a church raffle, grandmother poured it straight down the sink. She didn't want alcohol in the house. A Verity celebration has always been food, cups of tea and mineral water. If Dad celebrated that night, I rather fancy he'd have had a nice cup of tea."

7

Reflections on the Record

Verity, Verity, I say unto you,
How is it your wickets cost you so few?
— A batsman's soliloquy

Appreciations and accolades flowed in abundance after Hedley Verity's world record feat. The above rhyming couplet, from the *Nottingham Journal*, was typical of tributes paid to the bowler. Headline writers and newspaper sub-editors played on the fact that "Verity" means "truth". The definition is somewhat ironic considering the record was so far-fetched. The *Yorkshire Evening Post* pronounced, "Verity of Verities, all is Verity", while the *Sphere* said, "Truth is stranger than fiction. Truth is Verity. Therefore Verity is stranger than fiction." The *Sphere* added: "Magnus est Verity et praevalebit" – a reworking of the Latin "Magna est veritas et praevalebit" from the Book of Ezra in the Hebrew Bible, meaning "Truth is great, and it shall prevail". Frank Stainton, of the *Leeds Mercury*, simply called it "the greatest bowling performance cricket has ever known", adding: "Verity clearly stands head and shoulders above every other left hander in the country at present and is drawing attention to his claims for inclusion in the winter's touring side." Stainton predicted: "If this latest achievement has not booked his passage for him, I shall be very much surprised." The *Daily Sketch* also considered Verity's perfor-mance a nudge to the selectors. "Such a feat as Verity's cannot fail to bring him once again very strongly into the running for the Australian tour. There are several good judges who insist that the England XI is incomplete without him." The *Nottingham Journal* felt Verity's display "reminiscent of the halcyon days of Wilfred Rhodes at his best". However, the paper made clear that "even that great bowler had never achieved anything so amazing as this". The *Yorkshire Evening Post* said, "Verity, right at the start of his county career, is among the immortals", while the *Yorkshire Post* ventured into nautical territory when it posed the question, "Verity's pace?" and answered with the classic, "Ten Notts, of course". The *Post* also published a leader on Verity:

> *For the second time in his career Verity has taken all ten wickets in an innings. Such a feat may be only a picturesque accident; in such circumstances as yesterday's it is much more than that. It is a great piece of bowling which*

How the Nottingham Journal reported the 10 for 10.

*the Fates permitted, for once, to be as good as it possibly
could be. A slow left-hander is always likely to be
dangerous on a rain-affected wicket; being dangerous is
one thing, and disposing of a first-class batting side in this
decisive manner is quite another ... Verity does one thing
supremely well; he bowls the left-hander's "going-away"
ball irresistibly, as none has since his great predecessor.
There is another aspect of the matter: to take an opportunity with both hands, to make the utmost of it,
demands those qualities of resolution and self-certainty
on which greatness must be founded. In short, we have
reason to believe that we have not yet by any means seen
the best of Verity. If, as we all hope, he goes to Australia
this winter, the full revelation of his quality may be
"down under" there.*

Just as Verity's performance provoked editorial reflection,
so it drew comment from newspaper readers, with several
writing to the *Nottingham Journal* in the days that followed
the 10 for 10. The letters, naturally, had a Nottinghamshire
bias and the first to have their say was someone called
"Disgusted", whose opinions sparked a deal of debate:

*Sir,
The present Notts XI has been described as a team
without a tail. Anyone present, as I was, at the
Headingley ground this afternoon would have amended
the description, making it a team without a backbone.
I have followed the fortunes of Notts for more years than
I care to remember, but I shall waste no more time
watching the performances of the present team. So inept,
so puerile – one might say, so disgraceful – a display as
theirs in this match I have never seen in first-class cricket.*

Verity may be a competent bowler, but he is not in the same class with his great predecessor in the Yorkshire team, Rhodes, or with the late Colin Blythe, or with Parker (at his best) or Freeman as a slow bowler. The Notts "batsmen" (one has to put the term in inverted commas) simply gave themselves to him.

If these youngsters to whom the Notts committee have recently given caps are the best of the young entry, would it not be better to recall George Gunn and Payton and the genial Barratt for another season or so?

I hope the person or persons responsible for persuading Voce to leave his initial style of bowling to become an indifferent "swinger" are satisfied with their handiwork.

Finally, I understand the Notts captain wanted 200 sixes hitting last season. Might I suggest that a few humble ones and twos would be very acceptable this season.

"Disgusted", however, was in a minority. Most readers recognised Verity's brilliance and tempered their criticism accordingly.

L. R. Keating, of Nottingham, wrote:

Sir,
I also was present at Headingley all three days. Far from "Disgusted" being correct, we were fairly and squarely beaten. In addition, I saw a piece of bowling such as will never be repeated. Verity may not be a Blythe or Rhodes ordinarily, but he was on Tuesday.

If "Disgusted" is a sample of the club's supporters, it is a bad lookout for Notts cricket. His is an attitude which confers neither dignity nor decency on the game, and I hope the majority of cricket lovers will resent it.

Verity family collection

The grip that made history.

With regard to the youngsters, did he see Harris's stand with Walker at Trent Bridge against Yorkshire last year, and the same lad take six wickets for eighty at Manchester, or the way he kept his end up at the Oval, to say nothing of his first innings score in this match? How has Keeton managed to get a batting average of forty-odd and be an England candidate? What about GV Gunn's 86 at Worcester last week? Voce, with his "indifferent swingers", has taken eighty-odd wickets this year and is in the first five in the averages.

A. J. Allcock, of Edwalton, agreed:

*Sir,
I should like to refer to a letter from a person who signs himself "Disgusted".*

The letter in itself is hardly worth reading, much less
replying to, were it not for the fact that the majority of
members are heartily sick of those grumblers and grousers
who can see good in every team but their own, and who
always know exactly how the game should be played,
and what should have been done.
If the writer of the letter referred to knows so much
about cricket, I think that the Notts committee will
gladly arrange a day next week, when there is no county
match, in order that he can come to the wicket and
demonstrate how the game should be played, and I will
guarantee that all the team will be present.
May I remind him of 1901 when such giants of the game
as AO Jones, JA Dixon, W Gunn, G Gunn, J Iremonger
and J Carlin were all dismissed for 13 against Yorkshire?
Let us all support and encourage our county team in
reverses as well as successes, and at the same time give
praise to our opponents when they deserve it, as Verity
did last Tuesday.

Finally, Edith M. Butler, of Eastwood, declared:

Sir,
I have read in your correspondence column the letter of
"Disgusted" on Notts v Yorkshire.
Much as every supporter and follower of Notts – and
there are still many loyal ones, despite the fact of their
ghastly batting failure at Headingley – will be disap-
pointed after Verity's sensational performance, such
letters of public condemnation can serve no good purpose.
The reference to the Notts youngsters and their county
caps is the unwarranted injustice of a narrow-minded
person, who would do well to remember the countless

runs and boundaries these young players have saved by
their alertness in the field during the present season – a
fact which George Gunn, Payton and Barratt would be
the first to acknowledge in all fairness to youth.
Furthermore, the remark about the Notts captain and
sixes is worthless and childish. Every lover of cricket
enjoys watching big hitting and, as much as "Disgusted"
would welcome "humble twos and ones", some of us find
too many of them a trifle boring.
May I remind the writer that even county cricketers are,
at best, only human, and that human nature is by no
means infallible. Their failures in the realm of sport are
the property of the general public, whilst the average
individual who is not in the limelight can hide his
shortcomings from a not too sympathetic world, and so
escape unjust criticism.

Amid the weight of words written on Verity's feat, whether
by cricket correspondents or newspaper readers, one thing
stood out like a sore thumb – the lack of comment from
Verity. The Yorkshire press did not interview him, and his
only quotes were in the *Sporting Chronicle*, which simply
stated: "Seen after his fine feat, Verity said that all he could
hope for before lunch was to keep the batsmen quiet while
the moisture in the wicket was drying. 'Afterwards,' he went
on, 'it was a different matter. The sun came to my aid just
long enough to make things difficult and, well, I took
advantage of it. As the batsmen succeeded each other I was
able to get sufficient spin on the ball to prevent them settling
down. That is all the explanation I can offer.'"

Nowadays, if somebody took 10 for 10, there would be
reams of quotes from the horse's mouth. Newspapers would

publish special pull-outs and the player's friends and family would be interviewed. Today's cricketers are sought for their comments even after quite mundane performances: if, say, when a batsman has top-scored with 46 out of 217 for nine, or if a bowler has claimed his team's best figures of four for 45. The contrast is remarkable, the change in style revealing. Cricket writers of yore were neither encouraged to obtain player quotes nor expected to give more than their own observations, a concept that would be considered anathema by many journalists and sports editors now. Verity, in fact, was more widely quoted after his 10 for 36 against Warwickshire, as though there was a feeling he'd been there, done that and got the T-shirt in terms of recording a 10-wicket haul. Indeed, the sports pages of Wednesday 13 July 1932 gave more prominence to the fact the British Olympic team were that day departing for America than to Verity's world record. Coincidentally, given that record, it was the 10th Olympiad and 10th Street in Los Angeles was renamed Olympic Boulevard in honour of the Games.

As well as the lack of reaction from Verity, only one former cricketer was reported giving comment. Sir Stanley Jackson, the former Yorkshire and England all-rounder, who won all five tosses and topped the batting and bowling averages in the 1905 Ashes, described the feat as "the most brilliant I have known" while speaking at the opening of the new King's School in Pontefract, West Yorkshire. Sir Stanley said he'd been invited by a newspaper to contrast the cricket of today with the cricket of his era, but had declined, telling delegates: "If I had undertaken the task, I would have been able to say that I remembered nothing of my day which could possibly have beaten Verity's feat." His words occasioned "loud applause".

Verity was also back at school the day after taking 10 for 10. He joined a group of Yorkshire cricketers at Barnard Castle School, County Durham, alma mater of George Macaulay. Each year, Macaulay took a strong Yorkshire side to challenge the school in a gesture appreciated by staff and students. Verity claimed two wickets as Barnard Castle scored 193 for eight declared, Macaulay's men sailing to a seven-wicket win. Herbert Sutcliffe was not among them, however, for he was turning out for the Players – alongside Harold Larwood and Bill Voce – against the Gentlemen at Lord's. The trio had travelled to London by train straight after the Headingley match for one of the showpiece games of the season. Sutcliffe hit 16 in the Players' first innings 301, Larwood starring with four for 54 as the Gentlemen replied with 430 for eight declared. Sutcliffe scored 22 second time around as the Players were dismissed for 320, the match ending drawn. Although Yorkshire had no first-class game the day after Verity's 10 for 10, Nottinghamshire were back in action against Essex at Trent Bridge. After Arthur Carr lost the toss, his side made a sensational start, reducing Essex to 54 for eight as the Staples brothers ran amok. Sam took five for 50 and Arthur four for 47 as Essex were ejected for 147. When Nottinghamshire replied, Walter Keeton hit 141 and Carr – with the bat borrowed from Larwood – an unbeaten 132 before the hosts declared on 306 for five. George Vernon Gunn, whose second string leg-spin wasn't used at Headingley, returned a career-best seven for 44 as Essex responded with 98 to lose by an innings and 61 runs.

Verity's next cricket came on Friday 15 July, when he played for Yorkshire in their annual match against the Yorkshire Cricket Federation at Headingley. He took six for 26 from 10 overs in a game that finished drawn. Verity returned to first-class action the following day when Yorkshire hosted the Indians at Harrogate. He claimed five for 65 and two for 40 as Yorkshire prevailed by six wickets, Macaulay following his wicketless haul in the 10 for 10 with a career-best eight for 21 in the tourists' second innings.

The return match between Nottinghamshire and Yorkshire took place at Trent Bridge a fortnight after the 10 for 10. It was Sam Staples's benefit game and 17,000 spectators – Nottinghamshire's biggest crowd of the season – turned out for a man who'd foregone the honour the previous year to help raise funds for "Dodge" Whysall's widow. After winning the toss on a perfect pitch, Nottinghamshire scored more slowly than they had at Leeds. They made 168 in 108.1 overs, Verity recording two for 34 and Macaulay capturing five for 49. It had been 41 years since Yorkshire lost in Nottingham, and the *Yorkshire Post* reported that "the weight of every one of those years seemed to be on the home side's batsmen". After day two was washed out and the third rain affected, Yorkshire closed the game on 169 for six, achieving first-innings points by a single run. Verity scored 26 as nightwatchman before falling lbw to Sam Staples, who lost around £500 due to the weather (roughly £17,500 today). Yorkshire softened the blow with their own donation to his benefit fund – the magnificently apposite £10 10s.

The draw at Trent Bridge was the only Championship match Yorkshire failed to win between the 10 for 10 and the end of the season. In fact, they won 14 of their last 15 Championship games, a run that went back to 1 July. After their shocking start, when they sat second-bottom of the table after the first quarter, Yorkshire went unbeaten for the rest of the summer, winning 18 of 21 fixtures, including the last nine. As *Wisden* observed: "The contrast between the early fortunes of the side and the triumphant performances which characterised the efforts of the team subsequently was startling to a degree." Such consistency could hardly fail to bring the title, which Yorkshire won by beating Hampshire at Bournemouth in their penultimate match. It was their seventh Championship in 14 seasons since the war. In their final game, Yorkshire thumped second-placed Sussex by 167 runs at Hove, Verity taking six for 48 in the second innings as the home side lost for the only time that season. Although Yorkshire's title was richly deserved, with Brian Sellers's men finishing 53 points above their nearest rivals and winning five more matches, one London paper had provocatively claimed that "whilst Yorkshire's success as champions would be welcomed by three-quarters of the country, Sussex's would be acceptable to everyone".

There were no such noises north of the Trent, where Yorkshire's title was suitably saluted. The *Yorkshire Post* insisted: "Yorkshire's 16th County Championship triumph will always be reckoned, and with entire justification, as one of the most remarkable of them all", adding that "when the time comes for another volume to be added to those which contain the cricket history of the county, season 1932, because of its drama, its record-breaking performances and, above everything else, its grand cricket, will have a place all its own". That grand cricket was reflected in gate receipts, which totalled £10,178 4s 10d – £1,659 8s 4d more than the previous year. The most lucrative fixture was the Nottinghamshire match, which earned £1,100 5s 4d, the paying attendance of 19,807 Yorkshire's highest for a home game that season.

Nottinghamshire finished fourth in the Championship, seven points behind Kent, 21 behind Sussex and 74 adrift of

Yorkshire, losing just one of their last 13 games in a spirited response to their hammering at Headingley. *Wisden* felt they would have challenged more strongly for the title had Larwood and Voce played every match. However, due mainly to representative calls, Larwood missed four games and Voce five. Larwood still topped the national Championship averages with 141 wickets at 11.62, while Voce took 106 Championship wickets at 16.79. Larwood also headed the first-class list with 162 wickets at 12.86.

Nottinghamshire's batting was statistically impressive. Five players – Walter Keeton, Willis Walker, Arthur Staples, Arthur Carr and Charlie Harris – passed 1,000 runs, Keeton top-scoring with 1,680 at 42.00. However, it was felt that Nottinghamshire's batting still let them down, as it had done at Leeds. "While the records suggest no real limitations in the run-getting powers of the side, the explanation of the question why Notts did not make a closer fight for first honours is nevertheless probably to be found in the shortcomings of some batsmen on critical occasions," commented *Wisden*.

In contrast, Yorkshire invariably found someone to step up when needed. They also possessed, in Herbert Sutcliffe, the country's standout batsman by a distance. For the third time in five seasons, Sutcliffe scored more than 3,000 runs, his aggregate of 3,336 at 74.13 the highest of his career, and still the sixth-highest ever. The second-highest run-scorer in 1932 was Wally Hammond, way back on 2,528 at 56.17, while Yorkshire's next-best was Maurice Leyland with 1,980 at 52.10, his season redeemed by his four-figure August.

Just as Sutcliffe and Leyland led Yorkshire's batting, so Verity and Bill Bowes directed the bowling. Verity finished second in the first-class averages to Larwood with the same number of wickets (162) at 13.88, while Bowes came third with 190 at 15.14. *Wisden* said of Verity: "While preserving the power of spinning the ball and the command of length which had so distinguished his bowling twelve months earlier, Verity acquired a faculty of making the ball 'lift' and this development brought him lots of wickets, largely through batsmen giving catches in the slips or to the fieldsmen standing close in. Verity also improved in the art of 'flighting' the ball even if he was not quite master of that important side of bowling and his faster ball, delivered from a good height, was more accurate in direction than it had been in 1931."

Twelve days before Yorkshire clinched the Championship, Verity was picked for the tour to Australia. Yorkshire had four representatives in the 17-man squad, which included Sutcliffe, Leyland and Bowes, the latter selected at the 11th hour and given three days to pack and prepare. Verity's place was effectively booked on that thrilling Tuesday in mid-July when, having known that he'd need to do something special to make the tour, he simply recorded the sport's best figures. Under the headline "Rejoicings in Rawdon", the *Yorkshire Post* told of a village's pride:

> *Rawdon, the small home town of Hedley Verity, the Yorkshire bowler, was electrified last night when the news leaked out that Verity had been chosen to travel with the England touring side to Australia. At first there was incredulity and then open jollification, and the customary Sunday night sleepiness of the village was shaken off with a merry shrug. Villagers discussed the news from door to door, and assuredly had it been any other night but the Sabbath, the village band would*

*have been unceremoniously hauled on duty. Verity was
having one of his rare Sundays at home that his cricketing duties permit during the season, and as the news
spread he was inundated with good wishes. A Press man
was the first to break the news to him, and his first words
were typical of the modesty of this tall, shy, and rather
taciturn young Yorkshireman. "I hope to justify my
choice," he said, "and I shall try not to let the Old
Country down." He smoked his pipe quietly and was
obviously finding it difficult to describe his pride and
delight. "I am, naturally, delighted," he remarked, and
his face, full of smiles, spoke more eloquently than any
words could have done. "It is a great honour – one that
any man would be proud of." He refused to express
himself further. There were no airy promises from this
already fairy Yorkshireman, who, in two seasons, has
jumped from the insignificance of club cricket to the very
peak of international cricket. Although clearly excited he
adroitly turned the conversation into other channels, and
when brought back to the subject of the forthcoming
Australian tour, he smilingly answered question with
question. "What can I say?" he asked. "Come to me
when the tour is ended and then I may have something
to say." Was there something prophetic in his comment?
Yorkshire and England may be sure of this, in his own
words, Verity will not "let the Old Country down"!*

8

Verity's Decade

They came in their thousands to see Hedley Verity and his Yorkshire team-mates set off for Australia. Some 5,000 people packed Leeds station to bid them farewell and bon voyage. It was 16 September 1932 and Verity, Herbert Sutcliffe, Maurice Leyland and Bill Bowes were heading to London for the MCC dinner. From there it would be a short trip to Tilbury to board the *Orontes* for the eight-month tour. As they prepared to take the Pullman train south, a familiar figure stepped from the crowd. Bobby Peel, the 75-year-old former Yorkshire spinner, who'd called the young Verity "a good fast bowler wasted", approached the quartet with a box of white roses. The sprightly Peel gave each man a rose, shook him by the hand and wished him good luck. No sooner had the impromptu ceremony concluded than the train departed amid "a hurricane of cheers".

The voyage to Australia took 31 days. The boat went via Gibraltar, Toulon and Naples, steamed on through the Straits of Messina, the Suez Canal, Red Sea and Arabian Sea before docking at Ceylon en route to Fremantle. The studious Verity kept a tour diary, noting impressions of his first trip abroad. Suffused with wonder, like a wide-eyed schoolboy, he was stunned to discover "the ship is perfectly steady, just like an hotel" and described "endless interest in watching weather, fish, cloud, angles of sun, all strange to me". Verity savoured life aboard ship and threw himself into the various activities. There was a choir and cinema, dances and deck quoits, in addition to running and light fitness drills. Then, some 10 days into his great adventure, Verity received a summons. The England captain wanted to see him ...

Verity had formed a poor impression of Douglas Jardine. He'd had a disagreement with him over field positions for left-arm spinners when he'd played for England in 1931. Verity even told a friend he had doubts about touring under Jardine. Now Jardine locked his cabin door while they held a private tactical talk.

Tall and toffee-nosed, with icy demeanour, Jardine took some getting to know. Sutcliffe initially thought him "a queer devil", while Bowes confessed to forming "a dislike". Born in India, to a Scottish family, Jardine attended Winchester. Physical punishment was all around – as much part of life as morning assembly – and perhaps explained his cold exterior. A correct if cautious right-hand batsman, the 32-year-old had aquiline features. He wore a multi-coloured Harlequin cap and seemed to epitomise colonial arrogance. Jardine divided popular opinion and drew dissension wherever he went. On hearing of his appointment as captain, Rockley Wilson, an ex-Yorkshire player and one of his masters at Winchester, predicted: "We shall win the Ashes ... but we may very well lose a Dominion."

Jardine's desire to meet Verity was two-fold: he wanted to end any lingering tension and to outline Verity's role in the series. This was not to run through opponents as he'd done so dramatically against Nottinghamshire; instead, it was to be that of workhorse on pitches conducive to quicker bowlers. This would enable Jardine to rest and rotate his premier weapons, Harold Larwood and Bill Voce, who'd spearhead

Verity family collection

Yorkshire's four representatives on the Bodyline tour (l–r): Hedley Verity, Bill Bowes, Herbert Sutcliffe, Maurice Leyland.

England's style of attack. Jardine talked Verity through the same tactics he'd discussed with Larwood, Voce and Arthur Carr three weeks after the 10 for 10 game. He set out the strategy to combat Don Bradman, which would ultimately bear out Wilson's warning. This would see England's pace bowlers adopt a short leg stump line to restrict scoring chances to one half of the field, forcing batsmen to flirt with a packed leg-side ring. Jardine referred to the tactic as "leg theory". The world came to know it by the populist "Bodyline".

Bradman destroyed England in 1930, scoring 974 runs at 139.14 to help Australia to a 2-1 win. If England were to recover the Ashes, it was crucial that he was cut down to size – and at least kept in check by men such as Verity. After watching footage of the 1930 Oval Test, Jardine thought he

knew how to stop him. Detecting Bradman's discomfort
against Larwood, he saw how he flinched and backed away
to leg, one ball causing him to drop his bat after striking him
painfully over the chest. According to legend, Jardine
exclaimed: "I've got it! He's yellow!" Although Verity did
not especially like Bodyline, or savour the thought of a
containing role, he respected the reasoning that shaped the
strategy. In Jardine he sensed a kindred spirit, someone who
also took the game seriously. Jardine, too, saw something in
Verity – a mirror image of his scientific soul.

Bradman thought Verity might prove useful on "a suitable
wicket" but saw no place for him in the Test side. It wasn't
long before he knew he was wrong. In the second tour
match, between an Australian XI and MCC, Verity sent
back Bradman for three, caught at slip by Wally Hammond.

Douglas Jardine, Verity's great friend and captain, pictured at Scarborough in 1926.

Verity took seven for 37 in that game at Perth, where the Australians were forced to follow-on and eventually thankful to emerge with a draw. When England next came up against Bradman, playing for another combined team in Melbourne, Verity wasn't picked but perceived from the sidelines a chink in "The Don". In his tour diary, he recorded: "He was soon making some brilliant but rash shots, eventually being lbw to Larwood's good length one. He sat back expecting the bouncer. It looked to me as if he was rattled, a state of mind that may be a big help to us in the Test series."

Verity was chosen for the First Test in Sydney, where the harbour bridge had opened that March, built by the Yorkshire firm, Dorman Long. He didn't take a wicket in a 10-wicket win, Larwood returning 10 for 124 in a game that Bradman missed through illness. Verity's memory was mainly of the crowd, which "made more noise than I have ever heard outside an FA Cup final". One wag shouted, "Give Variety a go" in a witty play on the Yorkshireman's surname. Verity said it was "a bad match for me" and noted "the Australians didn't shape at all at the quick stuff bowled at leg and middle to a leg trap". He was replaced for the Second Test at Melbourne by Bowes, who stunned the crowd by bowling Bradman for a golden duck. Bradman gained revenge with a second innings century before Australia's spinners, Bill O'Reilly and Bert Ironmonger, sealed victory by 111 runs. Verity replaced Bowes for the Third Test at Adelaide, the match that ignited an incendiary tour. With tensions running high at England's tactics, Larwood hit Australia captain Bill Woodfull above the heart and wicketkeeper Bert Oldfield on the head, although neither ball was to a Bodyline field. Woodfull told England manager "Plum" Warner, "There are two teams out there

– one is trying to play cricket and the other is not", while the Australian Board of Control branded Bodyline "unsportsmanlike" in a threatening cable to MCC, a charge it withdrew. England won a match *Wisden* called "a disgrace to cricket" by 338 runs, Verity scoring 45 and 40 and managing one wicket – that of Bradman, caught-and-bowled.

Verity, who claimed Larwood's bouncer count was "not 10 in 25 overs", said England's players were subjected to "the worst demonstrations I have ever seen". He added they were constantly "counted out" and that Larwood "walked back to repeated boos and hoots from the crowd". After Jardine won a vote of confidence in his tactics, with the players reiterating support for him at a team meeting held at Jardine's request, Verity made a key contribution in the Fourth Test at Brisbane, where England clinched the Ashes with a six-wicket win. After Australia scored 340, England were 264 for eight when Verity joined Eddie Paynter, the Lancashire left-hander, who'd left hospital with tonsillitis and a 100-degree temperature in a selfless attempt to help out the side. They added 92 as England secured a narrow lead, Australia responding with 175 before England successfully chased 160. Verity's best bowling came in the last Test at Sydney, where he took three for 62 and five for 33, England's eight-wicket win sealing a 4-1 victory. In his four Tests in the series, Verity claimed 11 wickets at 24.63, finishing second in the averages only to Larwood. In all first-class games, Verity topped the averages with 44 wickets at 15.86.

The tour that tamed Bradman, who averaged 56.57 against an overall career average of 99.94, effectively finished Larwood and Jardine. Larwood refused to apologise for his bowling and never played for England again, while Jardine was ultimately ostracised by MCC and had retired before the

An iconic image from the Bodyline series as Australia captain Bill Woodfull ducks a bouncer from Harold Larwood at Brisbane.

next Ashes series. Although Jardine was shunned in the corridors of power, and loathed by some who followed the game, he was positively loved by many of his players. Sutcliffe changed his "queer devil" assessment to "one of the greatest men I have ever met", while Bowes performed a similar volte-face. Bowes admiringly concluded that Jardine "would have fought lions barehanded", while Larwood said simply: "I loved the man." Verity thought Jardine unrivalled as a captain, while Jardine felt Verity would have made a fine leader. "No captain could have a greater asset on his side than Verity," he wrote. "He would make a great captain himself." Verity grew to respect Jardine so much he named his second son after him; the first was named after Wilfred Rhodes.

Despite the fulminating fallout from Bodyline, which continued through 1933 and beyond, MCC kept Jardine as captain for the 1933–34 tour to India. Verity was the only other survivor from the Australia campaign as England rested most senior players. It was a good trip for Verity, who topped the Test averages with 23 wickets at 16.82. England won the three-match series 2-0 on their maiden Test tour to the region. Verity's best performance was in the last Test at Madras, where he took 11 wickets in the match, including seven in the first innings, but the apex of his Test career came later that year when cricketing rivalries resumed against Australia. In the Second Test of the 1934 series, Verity captured a then Ashes record 15 for 104 – including 14 for 80 on the third day, beating the previous best of 15 for 124 by Wilfred Rhodes at Melbourne in 1904. Verity claimed seven for 61 in the first innings and eight for 43 in the second to help England to victory by an innings and 38 runs. It was their first Test win over Australia at Lord's since 1896, and their only one against them there in the 20th century. Verity ripped through the Australians after overnight rain. Surveying soggy streets from the team hotel, he'd said at breakfast, "I shouldn't wonder if we don't have a bit of fun today. It looks as though it might turn a little." On his way to the ground, Verity ran over and killed a black cat, stopping to find the owner to offer his apologies. Jardine wrote that Verity's performance in this match "may possibly have been equalled, but certainly has never been surpassed", while Neville Cardus said Verity's "run to the wicket, so loose and effortless, was feline in its suggestion of silkiness hiding the claws". Cardus added: "The record-hunters will revel in his figures. And the gods of the game, who sit up aloft and watch, will remember the loveliness of it all, the style, the poise on light toes, the swing of the arm from noon to evening." Verity twice claimed the wicket of Bradman, caught-and-bowled in the first innings and held by wicketkeeper Les Ames in the second from a towering mis-hit straight above the stumps. Once Bradman departed, the Australians disintegrated, but summer belonged to the batting sensation. After totalling just 133 in the first three Tests, Bradman returned to form with 304 at Headingley and 244 in the last Test at the Oval, Australia running out 2-1 winners.

Of all the duels in his cricketing career, Verity chiefly relished those with Bradman. Lesser bowlers would have baulked at the thought; not many *relished* bowling at "The Don". The greatest batsman cricket has known, Bradman married panache with pragmatism. R. C. Robertson-Glasgow called him "that rarest of Nature's creatures, a genius with an eye for business". Born in the tiny community of Cootamundra, New South Wales, on 27 August 1908, Bradman was brought up in the country town of Bowral, about 70 miles south-west of Sydney. As a boy, he repeatedly struck a golf ball against a water tank with a cricket stump, the ball rebounding at varying angles in a practice routine that sharpened his reflexes. Just five foot seven, and physically unimposing, Bradman was blessed with rare determination. As *Wisden* put it, "He could be 250 not out and yet still scampering the first run to third man or long leg with a view to inducing a fielding error." Legend has it that Bradman called his 309 in a day at Leeds in 1930 "a nice bit of practice for tomorrow".

Verity was cut from comparable cloth and enjoyed the challenge of confronting the best. The Yorkshireman was similar to Sherlock Holmes: he liked major problems, not minor ones. Not for Verity the facile task of bamboozling batsmen on a turning pitch, the equivalent of Holmes undertaking to find a missing moggy on Baker Street. Verity's idea of heaven was bowling to

Getty Images

*Don Bradman pictured during his then
world record Test innings of 334 at
Headingley in 1930. "The Don" admitted
he was "never sure" with Verity, who
dismissed him more times than anyone in
Test cricket.*

Bradman on a surface like marble in strength-sapping heat; it
was akin to Holmes's desire to extend himself against Professor
Moriarty – even to the depths of the Reichenbach Falls. Verity
savoured the peril of the precipice. Like Moriarty to Conan
Doyle's sleuth, Bradman presented his paramount challenge, the
ultimate test of nerve and skill. Easy pickings were for the
Inspector Lestrades of the cricketing world, plodding Joes who
could no more appreciate the subtleties of bowling than Bradman
could bespoil the high arts of batting. Verity wanted a task for
his mind as well as his fingers.

Such was Verity's desire to develop himself, J. M. Kilburn said he was "genuinely sorry when Bradman had to miss a Test match". When Verity removed Bradman with his first ball at Melbourne in 1937, Kilburn said he was "almost disappointed", adding: "The catch at short leg was too much in the nature of a batting accident for Verity to savour full satisfaction. His pleasures were in the longer term, pleasures of the great opponent harassed to a final mis-hit or bullied to an error of momentary over-assurance. Verity wanted to work for Bradman's wicket, to develop a plan, to watch the closing of a trap." Verity himself had a saying: "Do not praise me when I have taken eight for 20 on a sticky wicket, but when I have got two for 100 on a perfect wicket." It raises the possibility that his 10 for 10 might not have meant more to him than some of his less remarkable analyses.

Verity's approach was strength and weakness. Kilburn, who watched him more than any other writer, said he sometimes over-complicated in pursuit of perfection. "There were times in county cricket when he appeared to be deliberately making the game harder for himself by insisting on achievement in a predetermined manner; when he seemed to spend three overs preparing an lbw snare against a batsman who, unharassed, would probably have mis-hit into the covers anyway." Kilburn said Verity sometimes became "'sicklied o'er with the pale cast of thought', and spent so much time in laying plans to deceive his enemies that he neglected to use the weapons the gods had given him, and ignored spin upon turning wickets to engage in the less obvious delights of a battle of wits". Kilburn felt Verity took time to recover from the Bodyline campaign and the containing role that Jardine commanded. He said Verity returned to county cricket with a "maiden-complex" and "appeared satisfied to permit batsmen to stay at the crease

providing they acknowledged themselves under his control".
Kilburn added it was only a passing phase and that "the
benevolent despot" soon became "the insistent conqueror".

Verity's taste for bowling at Bradman was swelled by his
striking record against him. Verity dismissed him eight times
in Tests – more than anyone else – and a record-equalling 10
times in first-class cricket along with Australian leg-spinner
Clarrie Grimmett. R. C. Robertson-Glasgow paid Verity the
signal compliment of saying that he alone kept Bradman's
Test average beneath 150 and felt he was "one of only three
or four bowlers who came to the battle with Bradman on not
unequal terms". Kilburn said honours between the two men
"were not so much divided as added together, bowling
enhanced by the power in the batting and batting elevated by
the skill and persistence in the bowling". Just as Verity
esteemed Bradman, so Bradman admired Verity. Bradman
said he was "never sure" with Verity and bemoaned the fact
"there's no breaking point with him". Bradman admitted he
could "never claim to have completely fathomed Hedley's
strategy, for it was never static or mechanical". Against
Verity, Bradman's Test average near-halved to 50.12, Verity
conceding 401 runs from the 932 balls he bowled to him.

Verity played 40 Test matches, taking 144 wickets at 24.37.
Seventeen of those games were against Bradman, although
Bradman was unable to bat at The Oval in 1938 after injuring
an ankle. That was Verity's last Ashes Test and one of the
most famous, England winning by an innings and 579 runs on
the back of Len Hutton's 364 to level the series 1-1, a result
that was insufficient to regain the Ashes after Australia over-
turned a 2-0 deficit in 1936–37. The 22-year-old Hutton
batted 13 hours and 17 minutes, faced 847 balls and struck 35
fours in a record total of 903 for seven declared, his innings

"*The style, the poise on light toes, the swing of the arm from noon to evening*" – *Neville Cardus on Verity in motion.*

Ron Deaton collection

beating the previous Ashes best of 334 by Bradman at Leeds in 1930 and Wally Hammond's world Test record 336 not out against New Zealand at Auckland in 1933. Verity and Hutton were friends; they played golf and Verity gave the young man driving lessons near his home in Pudsey. At The Oval, where Yorkshire had five representatives with Maurice Leyland, Bill Bowes and Arthur Wood also playing, Verity made a point of staying with Hutton during the lunch and tea breaks to ensure his concentration did not falter. Hutton said Verity's "quiet, natural dignity" was "an immense source of strength to me throughout those long hours", while Verity further eased Hutton's tension by taking him to Bognor Regis on the rest day of the game. They lunched with one of Verity's school friends and, in the afternoon, played cricket on the beach.

Verity's penultimate Test was on the 1938–39 tour of South Africa and one of cricket's most remarkable matches. England were 654 for five in the fifth and final game in Durban, chasing 696, when they had to halt their pursuit to catch the boat home. A thunderstorm had prevented play after tea on day 10, and England had to take the 8.05 p.m. train in order to reach Cape Town in time to board the *Athlone Castle*. Insufficient time therefore remained to complete the last timeless Test, in which Verity bowled a then Test record 95.6 eight-ball overs (766 deliveries) and took four wickets.

Just as Australia and Bradman governed Test cricket in the 1930s, so Yorkshire dominated the county cricket decade. In addition to their seven Championships, they twice finished third and were once joint-fifth. Yorkshire played 292 Championship matches during that period, winning 164 and losing 26. Verity played 228 of them and was on the losing side just 17 times.

If popular wisdom dictates that bowlers win matches, Yorkshire's titles were predominantly secured by Verity and Bowes. Between them they took 51% of the club's Championship wickets during the 30s, their most successful season being 1932, when their combined contribution climbed to 66%. Like Larwood and Voce they worked together, creating wickets for one another and sometimes turning batsmen round if one of them fancied a particular player. They discussed the game endlessly – Bowes was another of cricket's deep thinkers, a characteristic that cemented their friendship. Perhaps because of their dissimilar styles, the duo co-operated rather than competed. There was joy not jealousy at each other's triumphs, shared celebration with no hint of envy. Bowes might prosper against the top-order, prising open the door for Verity. They were the beating heart of a great Yorkshire side.

Hedley Verity and Bill Bowes, bosom buddies and the beating heart of a great Yorkshire side.

Ron Deaton collection

Usually they were favoured with the platform of runs. Yorkshire's batsmen scored swiftly and sizeably, affording scope to weave wicket-taking spells. The team played classic three-day cricket, recording big totals and defending them often. The component parts were a well-oiled machine. Superlative fielding backed up the bowlers. Under the strict instruction of Sellers, Yorkshire's fielders stood a yard closer to the bat than those of their rivals, ensuring shots that would not have carried to orthodox positions suddenly became conspicuous chances. Verity's chief accomplices were Arthur Mitchell (160 catches) and Arthur Wood (67 catches, 119 stumpings), who combined in 22% of his dismissals for the club. Mitchell was mostly gully to Verity, standing between square and a foot-and-a-half behind – sometimes barely a yard from the bat. The record "c Mitchell b Verity" was a standard scorebook entry of the period, the pair as synonymous in county cricket as Marks & Spencer in the world of commerce. Indeed, there was no greater irony when Verity took 10 for 10 than the fact Mitchell was off the field injured after being hit by Larwood. Verity himself was an excellent fielder, mainly in the slips or at short leg or gully. He took 269 catches in 378 first-class games.

Verity's analyses continued to astound. In 1933, on the Leyton ground where Holmes and Sutcliffe added 555 the previous year, he took 17 for 91 – still the joint eighth-best match figures of all time. Verity claimed all his wickets in a single day, a feat matched only by Colin Blythe (17 for 48 for Kent against Northamptonshire at Northampton in 1907) and Tom Goddard (17 for 106 for Gloucestershire against Kent at Bristol in 1939). In 1936, Verity took nine for 12 from 6.3 overs against Kent at Sheffield, the fourth-cheapest nine-wicket haul on record, the only wicket he didn't take being the first one of opening batsman Arthur Fagg, whom he caught off pace bowler Frank Smailes. Verity took six for 26 in the first innings too, his match return of 15 for 38 the second-best of his career. Along with his two 10-wicket performances, Verity claimed seven nine-fers, 13 eight-fers and 34 seven-fers, recording 164 five-wicket hauls and 10 wickets in a match 54 times.

The cheapest of those seven-fers was in his final first-class game in 1939, when he took seven for nine against Sussex at Hove. It was the last first-class match in England before the war and played in a surreal yet stubborn atmosphere. "The tension was awful," recalled the Sussex batsman George Cox. "There was a feeling that we shouldn't be playing cricket. Yet there was also a festive air. We knew that this was to be our last time of freedom for many years and so we enjoyed ourselves while we could."

Cox scored 198 as Sussex made 387 before Yorkshire closed a run-filled first day on 112 for one. The champions moved to 330 for three on a rain-hit day two, Hutton contributing 103. On 1 September, the final day, the news came through that Germany had invaded Poland, making war certain. At Old Trafford, Lancashire's match with Surrey was abandoned and all county games due to start the next day were cancelled. The Yorkshire committee wired Sellers to suggest that the Brighton fixture was called off too, but Sellers said that as it was a benefit game for Sussex's Jim Parks, the players would like to continue if possible. The request was agreed, and Yorkshire promptly lost their last seven wickets in the opening hour to finish 392 all out, Norman Yardley top-scoring with 108. Beneath a blazing sun, Verity was unplayable on a drying pitch as Sussex sank to 33 all out, the visitors easing to a nine-wicket win. With long distance train services having been cancelled, Yorkshire were forced to improvise transport. A green Southdown coach was arranged and, by mid-afternoon, the team were heading north through the quiet Sussex lanes. Kilburn, riding with them, recalled:

There was no guessing precisely what the future held, but there was no escaping the reflection that a well-loved

*way of life was being shattered, perhaps beyond repair.
The anxiety of the uncertain hung heavily in the air.
Scarcely anyone mentioned cricket, though the past few
days had brought cricket of uncommon quality. For a
mile or two the route led down the Great West Road
towards London. In that direction there was no other
traffic; the opposite path was crowded to danger point
with every conceivable kind of vehicle carrying every
conceivable cargo. Perambulators, bedding, household
goods, food hampers were piled on passing cars which
were hastening out of London as precaution against
bombing. Coach-loads of children swept by to unknown
foster homes. Urgency covered the earth. An experi-
mental blackout had been ordered throughout the
country for that Friday night and it was felt advisable not
to attempt to drive through the darkness. Like Cardinal
Wolsey on another significant journey, Yorkshire halted
at Leicester. Luggage was left in the coach overnight;
thoughts were beyond the creature comforts of shaving
tackle and a clean collar, and the journey was to be
continued soon after dawn. In any event there was little
sleep. Half the night was spent in awaiting delayed
telephone calls to explain revised arrangements, and
before eight o'clock on the Saturday morning Yorkshire
were in Yorkshire again. Halts began, one passenger
dropping off here, another there. Finally came journey's
end in City Square, Leeds, and thence departed their
several ways one of the finest county teams in the history
of cricket. It never assembled again.*

9

The Valiant End

Hedley Verity's father was waiting to meet him when he returned from his final fixture at Hove. No sooner had the team reached City Square, within the shadow of Leeds railway station, than he found his son in reflective mood. After shaking hands and exchanging pleasantries, they shared a conversation that came to be poignant. Following his son's death during the war, Verity senior wrote: "On his return from his last match at Brighton in 1939, I met him at the station. He greeted me with: 'This is the end of my cricket career.' I said, 'Nonsense, you have many years of cricket before you, even if this war lasts as long as the last.' He replied: 'I tell you, this is the end of cricket for me.' How many times have those words come back to my mind during the past weeks."

Verity junior saw war coming in 1937 and correctly predicted it would last six years. In 1938, at the time of the Munich Crisis caused by Germany's annexation of Czechoslovakia, he was reunited with an old acquaintance in the Headingley pavilion. Verity first met Lieutenant-Colonel Arnold Shaw of the Green Howards during the 1933–34 tour of India at a party after the Madras Test. Now he quietly took him to one side to ask how best he could serve his country. Shaw recalled: "Hedley asked my advice on what he could do and how best to prepare for it, if war should come. His profession prevented him from joining the

Territorial Army or any civil defence organisation, as his
cricket travels would make it impossible for him to fulfil his
obligations. So I made an alternative suggestion: I promised
and subsequently gave him a collection of military books,
advised him to study them and arranged that when war did
come he would get in touch with me."

Len Hutton remembered that Verity spent much of his free
time during the 1938–39 tour of South Africa eagerly devouring
these military manuals. He studied them with the same dili-
gence with which he applied himself to dismissing batsmen.
Army tactics and manoeuvres were assimilated as ardently as
Douglas Jardine's strategies to stop Don Bradman. Now
Verity had his sights on a different opponent – Adolf Hitler.

Verity's attitude to Hitler was simple. He recognised that he
had to be stopped. Verity's sister, Grace, recalled her
brother's warning as war approached. "This is no chuffing
garden party," he said. "This fellow Hitler means it if we
don't stop him. We have got to stop him." The peace-loving
Verity believed in the war. Colonel Shaw said his attitude to
the Germans was: "They started it, now let them take it."

Remarkably, just as Verity studied the workings of
warfare, so Hitler studied the laws of cricket. A few days
after the 10 for 10, the *Yorkshire Evening News* carried an
article headlined "Adolphe Hitler As I Know Him" by
Carel Hautman, published to mark the German elections of
1932. Hautman recalled that Hitler requested during the
First World War that a British prisoner write out for him
the laws of the game. Hitler even tried his hand at the sport
in a "friendly" between POWs and German soldiers.
However, Hautman made clear that Hitler studied cricket
"not because he had time to play games but because it might

prove good training for warfare". He said Hitler – although impressed with cricketing strategy – ultimately considered the game too soft. "To Hitler, cricket did not seem manly enough. Why, he wanted to know, did the batsmen wear pads on their legs and gloves on their hands? The knowledge that if the ball beat the bat it would produce a heavy bruise should make the batsman more alert and the temporary pain would be good training." Hautman, who claimed "it is men like Hitler that the world needs to drag it from its terrible lethargy", said the Nazi leader turned his back on the sport. "Eventually, Hitler dismissed cricket as serious training for warfare – and I am appalled to think what he would have said had he sat beside me at Lord's not so many days ago and seen the monotonous stops for bad light, tea and refreshments."

Verity joined up in October 1939 along with Bill Bowes. The cricketers, who'd done most things together, planned to take infantry commissions, but Bowes was unable after a knee operation and instead became a gunnery officer. He took part in the North Africa campaign and was captured at Tobruk in 1942, spending the rest of the war as a POW and losing four-and-a-half stone. Verity was gazetted in the Green Howards in the winter of 1939 and posted to 1st Battalion under Colonel Shaw. The regimental depot was at Richmond, North Yorkshire, and Verity helped train NCOs. He bowled to them in the nets after army training and fastidiously maintained his physical fitness. The young men idolised him and responded to his fair-minded leadership. A fellow Green Howards officer said: "There was short shrift for the man who shirked his duties but with others, the slow and persevering, he displayed infinite patience."

Several Yorkshire players passed through the depot, including Len Hutton, Herbert Sutcliffe, Maurice Leyland, Arthur Wood, Norman Yardley and Frank Smailes. It prompted Verity to assert: "I reckon we can put out a team from this depot to beat any county side in England – except Yorkshire, of course." Verity had little aptitude for drill and was not a natural soldier, Colonel Shaw observing that "to watch him stripping a Bren gun, you would think that he had two right hands, mainly consisting of thumbs". Verity's forte was in the theatre of tactics, which, according to Colonel Shaw, was due to his ability to appreciate and adapt to cricketing situations. Verity still found time for the odd game of cricket, and in the summer of 1940 he represented Catterick Garrison alongside former Nottinghamshire captain Arthur Carr. In 1941, he played several times in Northern Ireland after the battalion was posted to Omagh. Yardley was also part of the unit and he remembered the rough Irish pitches were "sometimes more suitable for foxhunting", Verity feasting on flummoxed club players. In his final appearance, Verity took eight for 55 in a 21-run defeat to a North-West Ireland XI.

It is a little known fact that Verity one other time took 10 wickets in an innings. It happened on 28 June 1941 during a flying visit back to Yorkshire, when he captured 10 for 51 for Rawdon against Earby at Rawdon in his last match in England. After Rawdon made 209 for nine declared, Verity routed the visitors for 136. He bowled 12.5 overs with one maiden, and five men were caught, two caught-and-bowled, two stumped and one lbw. Watching was his eight-year-old son, Douglas. "I can see him in my mind running into bowl. He was operating from the Emmott Arms end, and the match was in aid of the Red Cross, I think. It was a wonderful

Verity family collection

Rawdon Cricket Club, where Verity played his earliest cricket and where he claimed another 10-wicket haul in his last match in England.

performance, and it gave me an idea of what the 10 for 10 must have been like."

In early 1942, 1st Battalion was posted to India, from where it made its way to Egypt, via Persia and Syria, prior to the Sicily landings. While in India, Verity suffered so badly from dysentery that doctors advised a change of climate. However, he stubbornly insisted on re-joining his men despite not being fully fit. For the rest of his days, Colonel Shaw blamed himself for not demanding Verity go home. In Egypt, where the battalion carried out intensive training, the soldiers took time off one day to play a game of cricket in Cairo. Verity took five wickets against Gezira Sporting Club, and the Green Howards won in the last over. There was one last match before the Sicily invasion – Verity's final game of cricket. It took place at El Shatt, on the east bank of the Suez

Canal, against fellow British servicemen, Verity returning six
for 37 to seal another win.

The Green Howards launched their attack on German
positions at Catania, Sicily, in the early hours of 20 July
1943. The 1st Battalion was part of the Allied effort and
attached to Eighth Army led by General Montgomery.
Eighth Army's objective was to capture the south-east of
the island, its airfields and ports. Italian defences were soon
swept aside but German ones – featuring crack troops from
Hermann Goering Division – put up better resistance. The
attack began with a heavy bombardment of the Plain of
Catania, low-lying land dotted with water channels against
the soaring backdrop of Mount Etna. B Company led the
Green Howards' offensive and Verity was its commander,
responsible for around 100 soldiers. After the initial attack,
Verity and his men crawled towards the enemy through
fields of corn under cover of moonlight. Tracer bullets
whizzed over their heads and mortars landed all around
them, setting fire to the corn as they crept. Although B
Company proceeded as planned, supporting companies
were less successful and Verity's men became exposed. In a
desperate attempt to salvage the situation, he ordered a
platoon to try to take the enemy's strongest point, a nearby
farmhouse, and another to give covering fire. Almost immediately, Verity was hit by flying shrapnel and his second-in-
command, Lieutenant Laurie Hesmondhalgh, killed
outright. As he lay in agony amid blazing corn, bleeding
profusely from a gaping chest wound, Verity instructed his
men to "keep going" and to "get them out of the farmhouse
and get me into it". But it was no good ... At around
4.30 a.m., B Company began to fall back and the stricken
Verity was trapped with his batman, Private Tom

Rennoldson, behind enemy lines. A fresh-faced fellow with chiselled cheekbones and mousy brown hair, Rennoldson, from Durham, had been Verity's batman for almost three years. Their bond transcended the confines of rank and Rennoldson nursed his captain while sending for a stretcher. It never came ... When dawn broke on the Catanian plain, illuminating a battlefield strewn with bodies, Verity and Rennoldson were swiftly captured. Verity was hoisted on to a broken mortar carrier, cushioned with corn, and taken to a makeshift field hospital about a mile away, where he underwent an emergency operation. When they lifted him on to the operating table, a grenade fell from his shirt and Rennoldson was ordered to unprime it. Later, Rennoldson was allowed to share a tin of soup with his captain before the Germans sent him to a POW camp in Austria. He never saw Verity again.

Along with fellow British prisoners, Verity was taken in an open railway truck through Sicily and on through the Straits of Messina, a narrow section of water between the eastern tip of Sicily and the Italian mainland. Eleven years earlier, he'd travelled this same stretch with his England team-mates en route to Australia for the Bodyline tour. Now his destination was the city of Reggio, where the prisoners spent one night in a military hospital. The following day, they were bundled on to a straw-covered goods train and taken to Naples – a journey that took almost two days. During this time, Verity fell increasingly ill and feverish. His bandages were filthy and his wound became infected. The prisoners were taken first to a German hospital, but it was full so they were moved to the military hospital at Caserta, some 16 miles away. Verity was in excruciating pain and part of a rib was pressing on his lung. He underwent another operation and part of the rib was removed using only a local anaesthetic. The operation seemed successful and Verity talked enthusiastically of repatriation, proudly showing fellow prisoners a photograph of his wife and two sons. However, he suffered three haemorrhages and, on 31 July 1943, 11 days after he'd been wounded, he died. Tragically, the Sicily campaign was to have been his last action as it had been intended to withdraw him from active service.

Some 100 miles away, at Chieti prisoner of war camp on the Adriatic coast, Bill Bowes chanced to hear of Verity's death from a Canadian airman, who'd been shot down over Naples a few days earlier. "Say, there was some cricketer guy at Caserta," said the airman innocently. The Canadian hesitated over the name before recalling: "Verity ... yeah, that's right, Verity." Anxious for news of his dear friend, Bowes enquired: "Do you mean Hedley Verity was in hospital at Caserta?" "Yeah, that's the fellow," said the airman. "But he's not in hospital now. He was buried yesterday. He must have been some important guy. The Italians gave him full military honours." Bowes staggered into the deserted roadway that ran through the camp. Pain sliced through the pit of his stomach. "The wind was cold but I did not notice it. For a long while I walked up and down that road, time stilled, living again the many incidents and hours we had shared together."

Back home, it was reported that Verity was wounded and missing. The Verity family spent an anxious August awaiting updates. Finally, confirmation came on 1 September that he'd died. It was four years to the day that he'd bowled his last ball for Yorkshire at Hove. "I will never forget the sight of father's face when he received the news of the death," said

Verity family collection

One of the most poignant photographs ever taken: Kathleen Verity and Hedley Verity senior listen as Private Tom Rennoldson recounts Captain Hedley Verity's harrowing last days in Sicily.

Verity's sister, Grace. "We had been assured that Hedley had been picked up and was a prisoner of war, and then came the letter from the Red Cross to tell us that he had died in hospital."

The news shocked Yorkshire and the cricketing world. Wilfred Rhodes wrote to the family: "I know you were proud of him. He was worth it, and that makes it all the harder to bear." In another message, George Hirst told them: "I am so glad that I knew him so well and will cherish his memory as long as I live." The following spring, Brian Sellers led tributes in the *Wisden* almanack: "His character and disposition never changed amidst all his many triumphs; he just remained Hedley Verity. I feel honoured to have met and played with him." In the same edition, R. C. Robertson-Glasgow supplied an epitaph that spoke for an empire: "His dignity was not assumed; it was the natural reflection of

*"In all that he did, till his most
gallant end, he showed the vital fire,
and warmed others in its flame".
R.C. Robertson-Glasgow's perfect
epitaph for the perfect sportsman.*

mind and body harmonised
and controlled. He was solid,
conscientious, disciplined;
and something far more. In
all that he did, till his most
gallant end, he showed the
vital fire, and warmed others
in its flame."

In the months and years
after Verity's death, people
speculated what he might
have accomplished had he
lived. He'd have been almost
41 at the start of the 1946
season, when Championship
cricket in England resumed,
past it by contemporary standards but not by those of the
1940s. Although the war would have cost him a wealth of
wickets, it would not have robbed him of his natural talent.
Arthur Mitchell felt Verity would have played for another
decade and formed the bedrock of the post-war Yorkshire
side with Len Hutton. Others felt he'd have become
Yorkshire captain and possibly England captain. J. M.
Kilburn believed cricket "lost an enormous influence for
good" and thought Verity would have been "influential in
the councils of cricket". Verity's son, Douglas, believed his
father would have stayed in the army as he savoured the
camaraderie and teamwork, while Verity himself raised an
interesting possibility. During his days in Northern Ireland,
he'd told a friend: "After the war, I would like to go into
politics to make this world a better place to live in."

Whether or not Verity would have returned to cricket, and perhaps to further 10-wicket hauls, the statistics show he was one of the greatest bowlers who ever lived. In a career of just nine years, he took 1,956 wickets at 14.90, by far the best average of his time. Of the 38 men who have taken more than 1,900 first-class wickets, Verity's average is second only to Alfred Shaw, the Nottinghamshire slow bowler of the 19th century, whose 2,027 wickets came at 12.12. However, Shaw played on more bowler-friendly pitches and had a first-class career-span of 34 years. Verity, in contrast, flourished in a decade dominated by batsmen. His total included 1,558 first-class wickets for Yorkshire at 13.70, including 1,304 County Championship wickets at 13.20. He topped the national averages in his first and last seasons and never finished lower than fifth.

Statistics, of course, are all well and good but they overlook in Yorkshire a fundamental question: who was better, Verity or Rhodes? The answer, alas, is blowing in the wind and definitive judgements impossible. Verity averaged 14.90 against Rhodes's 16.72, whereas Rhodes took more wickets and had greater longevity. Verity also bowled to a bloke called Bradman. "People argue whether my Dad or Wilfred was the best, but you can only be the best in your own time," said Douglas Verity. "My Dad bowled on the batting paradises of the 1930s, whereas Wilfred bowled on less well-prepared pitches. Dad was more versatile because he could bowl slow or medium-pace. But, then again, I'm prejudiced."

On the fifth anniversary of the outbreak of war, Rhodes umpired a memorial match for Verity at Roundhay Park, Leeds, along with Emmott Robinson. The game between Herbert Sutcliffe's Yorkshire XI and Jack Appleyard's XI

was ruined by rain but raised several thousand for the Red
Cross and local charities, plus £1,000 to endow a Hedley
Verity bed at Leeds General Infirmary. Sutcliffe's side
featured five men who'd played in the 10 for 10 match in the
form of himself, Arthur Mitchell, Maurice Leyland, Wilf
Barber and Arthur Wood, while Appleyard's contained
another in George Vernon Gunn. A prominent figure in
Yorkshire cricket, Appleyard organised many matches at
Roundhay Park in the war and his side for this one included
several Test stars, including Wally Hammond. One man
who'd dearly love to have been there was Verity's great
friend and captain Douglas Jardine, who'd been posted to
India after serving at Dunkirk. Jardine had been lucky to
survive in France after becoming detached from his men
only to be spotted and shown to a waiting destroyer. "We're
bound to be all right now, Sir," said his batman, "she's named
after your favourite bowler."

The ship was called HMS *Verity*.

A Feat Without Equal

Throughout the writing of this book I have feared waking up one day to find that someone, somewhere has beaten Hedley Verity's 10 for 10. Perhaps in some fixture in farthest Zimbabwe, or some meaningless match on the Indian subcontinent. *10 for 10: Hedley Verity and the Story of Cricket's Greatest Bowling Feat* could become the story of cricket's second-greatest bowling feat, its third-greatest, and so on. Such is the risk when writing about records, even those that may never be broken. However, there is no more striking aspect of the 10 for 10 than the fact that it stands so apart from its rivals. There have been over 50,000 first-class games, and up to four times as many individual team innings, and yet Verity's record is far out in front. What happened at Headingley on 12 July 1932 was not so much phenomenal as preternatural, a performance that positively defied explanation. To paraphrase cricket historian David Frith's observation of Don Bradman, the 10 for 10 record is not one in a million, it is much rarer than that.

Just how rare is evident first from the list of 10-wicket hauls. At the time of writing, there have been only 80 in first-class cricket, including two in the mid-19th century for which there is no record of the runs conceded, plus three accomplished in 12-a-side games. Such is Verity's pre-eminence, only George Geary, the man whose 10 for 18 he beat, also conceded fewer than 20 runs. The third-best analysis on record is 10 for 20 by Premangsu Chatterjee, a left-arm medium-pacer for Bengal against Assam at Jorhat in 1957, followed by leg-spinner Bert Vogler's 10 for 26 for Eastern Province against Griqualand West at Johannesburg in 1906. The only others to have conceded less than 30 runs all returned figures of 10 for 28. They were pace bowler Albert Moss, for Canterbury against Wellington at Christchurch in 1889, medium-pacer Bill Howell, for Australians against Surrey at The Oval in 1899, and pace bowler Naeem Akhtar, for Rawalpindi B against Peshawar at Peshawar in 1995. Verity's 10 for 36 against Warwickshire at Headingley in 1931 is also the joint ninth-best analysis of all-time. He is the only man to feature twice in the top 10.

If the 10 for 10 is the Everest of 10-fers, a performance that towers above other high peaks, its supremacy is swelled by the fact that no one has even endangered its summit. In no subsequent 10-wicket haul was the bowler in position to have beaten Verity; e.g., if he had nine for five before ending with figures of 10 for 28. The same is true of those who have taken nine-wicket hauls. The best nine-fer since Verity was leg-spinner Ahad Khan's nine for seven for Railways against Dera Ismail Khan at Lahore in 1964. However, Khan's wicket-taking sequence was ruined by a run out in a game Railways won by a record margin of an innings and 851 runs. The next best nine-fer was by Verity himself – nine for 12 against Kent at Sheffield in 1936, when he took the last nine wickets. No one, in fact, has taken the first nine wickets for less than 10 runs to give themselves chance of beating the record. Even other outstanding analyses such as Jim Laker's eight for two for England against The Rest at Bradford in 1950 did not threaten it; the score was 10 for one when Laker came on to bowl, Trevor Bailey having dismissed David Sheppard.

Verity's record seems more remarkable as time goes by. Nowadays, 10-wicket hauls are rarer than hen's teeth, never mind those at such low cost. Again, at the time of writing, there have only been four in the 21st century, the last in England by Ottis Gibson, the former West Indies pace bowler and England bowling coach, who took 10 for 47 for Durham against Hampshire at Chester-le-Street in 2007. Gibson's was the first 10-fer in England since swing bowler Richard Johnson's 10 for 45 for Middlesex against Derbyshire at Derby in 1994, itself the first in Championship cricket since seamer Ian Thomson's 10 for 49 for Sussex against Warwickshire at Worthing 30 years earlier. The feat is even more infrequent in Test cricket. Only two men have taken 10 in a Test innings, off-spinner Laker returning 10 for 53 against Australia at Old Trafford in 1956 and leg-spinner Anil Kumble 10 for 74 for India against Pakistan at Delhi in 1999. Laker also took nine for 37 in the first innings to finish with figures of 19 for 90. He is the only man to have taken more than 17 wickets in a first-class match.

The main reason 10-wicket hauls have become scarce is that modern pitches are covered. For all that Verity's record was not due to the pitch, he could not, as *The Times* made clear, "have accomplished his outstanding success without its aid", even if it was "only an accessory after his flight and length, which continually made the batsmen play the strokes they did not wish to after the ball had pitched". In Verity's day, spin bowlers flourished on rain-affected wickets and many exceptional analyses were recorded. Quicker bowlers, too, could be more of a handful, with the uncovered surfaces in striking contrast to the placid pitches made possible today by improvements to drainage and groundsmen's equipment. However, an important part of any 10-wicket performance is luck, and just as bowlers had more chance of taking 10 on uncovered pitches, so, of course, did their colleagues. The chances of George Macaulay – one of the greatest spin bowlers of his era – not taking a wicket at Headingley in 1932 while Verity ran riot were remote. When one considers all the genuinely sticky pitches in Verity's time, it becomes even more pertinent that no one – particularly a spinner – has challenged his crown. In those days, spinners would often open the bowling and had more chance of taking a 10-wicket haul; nowadays, the best they can normally hope for is an over before lunch, perhaps after pacemen have made early inroads.

Just as Verity's 10 for 10 sounds flawless, as though fashioned by heavenly not human hand, so the man himself seems too good to be true. Verity emerges from history with a halo; it's as if his analysis reflected his character. Accounts of Verity's gallantry as a soldier and goodness as a person suggest someone who should be beatified before being installed in the ICC Hall of Fame. Although the aching poignancy of his death might have softened perceptions, enshrouding his story in a saintly white, it seems Verity was genuinely that rarity of rarities: a man of whom no one had a bad word to say. "I don't think I have ever played with as fine a sport and as fine a gentleman as he," wrote Herbert Sutcliffe, while the Gloucestershire and England batsman Charles Barnett, one of Verity's best friends, said, "Hedley was especially a man whom men liked and respected. He seemed to bring the best out of others by his own personal example." The great George Hirst put it like this: "Anyone who came into contact with Hedley had but one thought: he may be a good bowler, but he is certainly a fine man."

Verity was no saint but he was a Christian. He attended church throughout his life and occasionally spoke at sportsmen's services. At one service in Skipton in 1931, he outlined his creed to the congregation: "Christianity is the only force, the only thing that can change the hearts of men. If you wish to help this old world to become a better place, your place is in the Christian church. There is a great deal of Christianity outside the church, but the church is carrying the flag." According to Colonel Shaw, Verity was "a fine example of the real Christian". Colonel Shaw added: "He was a man of clean living and clean speaking, charitable and quick to help others. He was a man's man, strong and full of courage."

Hedley Verity was virtuous and valiant, qualities that shaped the saintly image, but he had a frolicsome, fun-loving side. He was never virtuous to the point of vapidity and possessed a spirited sense of humour. Douglas Verity said: "Dad was serious on the pitch but off the field he was very jolly. He was a great practical joker and he'd creep up behind people and drop tins and things, making them leap out of their shoes. Dad was great at taking people off and quick to recognise their little quirks. Len Hutton said he used to make him laugh all the time with his shrewd observations of people." Verity's wit could be Yorkshire-dry. It was cut from the cloth of the county dressing room. "Dad once teased Charlie Barnett," said Douglas. "One day he said, 'Will you be coming to Australia with us, Charlie?' 'Why do you say that, Hedley?' said Charlie. 'What about so-and-so, and so-and-so? They're doing well, so why would the selectors pick me?' Dad said, 'No, I can get them out in five

overs and it takes me seven to get you, so they'll pick you.'"
According to Douglas, the ribbing was followed by warm
high-pitched laughter. "Dad always seemed to be laughing
or singing; I can never remember him downcast or sad."

Douglas was 10 when his father died. Hedley Verity
senior died not long afterwards, while Hedley's wife,
Kathleen, never recovered. The Veritys married in 1929;
their parents had pushed them out in their prams when
Kathleen's family lived in Headingley. The Metcalfes also
moved out to Rawdon, where Kathleen and Hedley were
reunited. Five foot nine, with curly dark hair, Kathleen was
Hedley's tower of strength, devoted to him and their two
children. "Mother never got over father's death; it hit her
incredibly hard," said Douglas. "Perhaps because we never

Verity family collection

had a funeral, I don't
think she ever accepted
he'd gone." Kathleen raised
Douglas as best she could
and his elder brother,
Wilfred. She played an
active part in the Rawdon
British Legion – she was
Branch standard-bearer of
the women's section – but
her health declined after
Hedley's death and she
died of cancer in 1956, aged
52. Nineteen years later,
Wilfred died in tragic
circumstances while walking
with his seven-year-old son,
also called Hedley, near

*Verity's eldest son, Wilfred, who
was tragically killed by a runaway
cattle trailer.*

their home in Otley, West Yorkshire. A cattle trailer towed by a Land Rover broke free, careered on to a footpath, crashed into young Hedley and crushed his father against a parked van. Wilfred, 43, a photographer and member of the local angling club, died of multiple brain injuries, while Hedley sustained a fractured skull but fully recovered.

The childhood memories of Douglas Verity cast precious light on his father's character. Mindful of the time he spent playing cricket, his father embraced family life whenever he was back in the bosom of loved ones. "What he did, looking back, was to try to fill our days with excitement and as many different things as he could because it was so rare he was with us," said Douglas. "He was always interesting, always entertaining, and there was never a dull minute when he was around." There was a vibrant quality to Verity the parent, a joyfulness and joie de vivre. "He'd come into the house and, if there was a bowl of fruit nearby, there'd be a very accurate stream of fruit going through the air at you and you'd be trying to catch pears and apples and bananas," said Douglas. "One of the things I remember vividly is that he used to have this curved, jewelled dagger that was given to him by the Nawab of Pataudi. Dad used to put it between his teeth and chase my brother around the house with it." Verity sometimes took Douglas and Wilfred for walks on the moors, combining exercise with education. He deliberately took them to featureless parts, away from the car, and made them find their own way back. "He taught us to know where north was from the green side of a rock or tree," said Douglas. "There was always a purpose behind what he did." Another story took similar lines … "When I was about five," said Douglas, "I had to go to kindergarten and it was a mile-and-a-half across three major roads. My mother was holding my hand, ready to go, and Dad said, 'Where are you going, Kathy?' 'I'm taking Douglas to school.' 'Has he been before?' 'Yes, he's been twice.' 'Then he must go on his own.' He was independent, you see, and he wanted us to be too." One of Douglas's favourite memories was of his father taking him into the England dressing room during the 1938 Ashes Test at Headingley. His father got him to show his forward defensive shot to the players, prompting the comment that the five-year-old was the better batsman. "When the match began, I was apparently more interested in playing with a toy than watching the cricket," said Douglas. "The only thing I remember about the game was suddenly hearing this loud cheer go up. 'What was that for?' I asked my mother. 'Oh,' she said, 'your Dad's just got Fingleton out.'"

Douglas's last contact with his father was when he and his brother received a letter in the war. The contents sounded as much personal credo as parental command and simply stressed: "Always remember to do what's right, and to fight for what's right if necessary."

Douglas was no mean cricketer himself, shining as an opening batsman in the Bradford League before a knee injury wrecked a promising career. He was also a fine golfer and became professional at Pwllheli Golf Club in North Wales, where many benefited from his kindly manner and coaching expertise. Rock climbing was another great love and Douglas for many years was deputy leader of the mountain rescue team in Snowdonia. One of his best friends was the English climber Joe Brown, while he also knew Sir Edmund Hillary and Sherpa Tenzing, along with others involved in the 1953 British expedition that conquered Mount Everest. The Everest team used Pen-y-Gwryd Hotel, at Nant Gwynant at the foot of Snowdon, as a training base, and Douglas managed the hotel when he first moved from Yorkshire in 1961. It was there, too, that he met his beloved wife, Ann, with whom he had two children, Charlie and Jamie. Both continued the cricketing tradition: Jamie played several matches for Wales while Charlie represented Caernarvonshire. Douglas thus had a father who played cricket for England and a son who played cricket for Wales.

Last year, 2013, marked the 70th anniversary of his father's death, a tragedy that continues to touch and inspire. Sadly, it was an anniversary that Douglas did not live to witness. On 24 August 2012, after a long and courageous battle with cancer, he died at the age of 79. Only a short time earlier, I'd interviewed him for this project and was inspired by his enormous support and encouragement; it was his dying wish that this book should be written.

Today, the name of Hedley Verity lives on. The exhibition of memorabilia at Headingley in 2005, which marked the 100th anniversary of his birth, was a huge success, as was a similar event at Hove in 2009, which marked the 70th anniversary of his last match for Yorkshire. The guest list included families of those who took part in the game, including that of Jim Parks, while Douglas gave a moving talk on his father's life. Also in 2009, a blue plaque was unveiled at Verity's birthplace, while, in 2010, J. D. Wetherspoon opened The Hedley Verity pub in Leeds city centre. The bar, which features photographs of Verity and cricketing contemporaries, is somewhat ironically entitled

Verity's son, Douglas, and the former Yorkshire and England all-rounder Brian Close celebrate the unveiling of a blue plaque to mark Verity's birthplace near the ground where he took 10 for 10.

The last resting place of Captain Hedley Verity.

given that Verity hardly imbibed; "Dad would have thought that hilarious," felt Douglas.

The proud name of Hedley Verity, however, is most prominently and poignantly displayed at Caserta, where he is one of more than 700 servicemen buried in the town's military cemetery. In 2008, the Commonwealth War Graves Commission approached Douglas to ask if he would like a new headstone and inscription above the grave. Beneath his father's name and date of death, he decided on the following tribute: "Gentle Man of Action ... Not Forgotten." "Gentle Man of Action" was the title of an article that appeared in *The Cricketer* in 2001.

Douglas never visited his father's grave. He feared it would have been too upsetting. There was talk of his going in the 1990s as part of an official party from Yorkshire County Cricket Club, but he pulled out. "The more I thought about it, the more I knew I couldn't face it."

In September 1954, a delegation did make the pilgrimage to Verity's resting place. Its members were en route to Australia for an Ashes series England won 3-1 – their first triumph Down Under since Verity toured in 1932–33. Those paying their respects were the England captain Len Hutton, his Yorkshire team-mates Bob Appleyard and Vic Wilson, the former Yorkshire pace bowler Abe Waddington, the Middlesex batsman Bill Edrich, the Surrey twins Alec and Eric Bedser plus several journalists, including Jim Kilburn and Bill Bowes. At dawn, the *Orsova* docked in the Bay of Naples and, by mid-morning, the men on a mission of tribute had taken two taxis to the tree-lined cemetery. Slowly, respectfully, they made their way through the low-cut lawns and pristine paths, shaded by the watching hills, as they sought the grave of the man who took 10 for 10. Kilburn captured the moment:

> Brief search along the soldierly ranks of marble head-
> stones brought us to Hedley Verity's grave. Among the
> flowers already growing there Len Hutton placed a
> spray of white roses fastened together with a Yorkshire

tie. He said nothing. Nothing needed to be said. We who knew Hedley remembered sharply. We took photographs, we left sign of our pilgrimage in the visitors' book and, as the burning sun of Italy climbed into the noontide sky, we turned away from the garden of quiet to the dust and glare of the road to Naples.

Appendices

The 10 for 10 Scorecard

NOTTINGHAMSHIRE

W. W. Keeton b Rhodes	9	–	c Macaulay b Verity	21
F. W. Shipston b Macaulay	8	–	c Wood b Verity	21
W. Walker c Barber b Bowes	36	–	c Macaulay b Verity	11
*A. W. Carr c Barber b Verity	0	–	c Barber b Verity	0
A. Staples b Macaulay	3	–	c Macaulay b Verity	7
C. B. Harris lbw b Leyland	35	–	c Holmes b Verity	0
G. V. Gunn b Verity	31	–	lbw b Verity	0
†B. Lilley not out	46	–	not out	3
H. Larwood b Leyland	48	–	c Sutcliffe b Verity	0
W. Voce b Leyland	0	–	c Holmes b Verity	0
S. J. Staples b Leyland	0	–	st Wood b Verity	0
B 8, l-b 6, w 2, n-b 2	18		B 3, n-b 1	4

1-15 2-35 3-40   (132.2 overs) 234
4-46 5-67 6-120 7-159 8-233
9-233 10-234

1-44 2-47 3-51   (47.4 overs) 67
4-63 5-63 6-63 7-64 8-64
9-67 10-67

First Innings – Bowes 31–9–55–1; Rhodes 28–8–49–1; Verity 41–13–64–2;
Macaulay 24–10–34–2; Leyland 8.2–3–14–4. *Second Innings* – Bowes 5–0–19–0;
Macaulay 23–9–34–0; Verity 19.4–16–10–10.

YORKSHIRE

P. Holmes b Larwood	65	–	not out	77
H. Sutcliffe c Voce b Larwood	0	–	not out	54
A. Mitchell run out	24			
M. Leyland b Voce	5			
W. Barber c and b Larwood	34			
*A. B. Sellers b A. Staples	0			
†A. Wood b Larwood	1			
A. C. Rhodes c A. Staples b Voce	3			
H. Verity b Larwood	12			
G. G. Macaulay not out	8			
W. E. Bowes not out	1			
B 5, l-b 5	10		B 4, l-b 4	8

1-1 2-37   (9 wkts dec. 62 overs) 163
3-122 4-123 5-125 6-128 7-135
8-152 9-154

(no wkt, 40.4 overs) 139

First Innings – Larwood 22–4–73–5; Voce 22–2–52–2; S. J. Staples 7–2–8–0;
A. Staples 11–3–20–1. *Second Innings* – Larwood 3–0–14–0; Voce 10–0–43–0;
S. J. Staples 18.4–5–37–0; A. Staples 6–1–25–0; Harris 3–0–12–0.

Umpires: H. G. Baldwin and W. Reeves.

The 10 for 10 Cast

The Yorkshire Side

Percy Holmes

Full name: *Percy Holmes*

Born: *25 November 1886, Oakes, Huddersfield*

Died: *3 September 1971, Marsh, Huddersfield*

Role: *Right-hand batsman, occasional right-arm medium-pace bowler*

First-class playing career: *1913–1935*

Test record: *Matches 7, Innings 14, Not outs 1, Runs 357, Average 27.46, Highest score 88, 50s 4; Catches 3*

First-class record: *Matches 555, Innings 810, Not outs 84, Runs 30,573, Average 42.11, Highest score 315*, 100s 67, 50s 141; Wickets 2, Average 92.50, Best bowling 1-5; Catches 342*

What happened next: Holmes missed the latter stages of the 1932 season with a knee injury that effectively ended his career. He managed only one more summer for Yorkshire with little success and returned to the Huddersfield mills where he'd worked as a youngster. Holmes played league cricket for Ebbw Vale and Swansea in the Welsh League before the war and had one season as a first-class umpire in 1947. He spent 11 summers as cricket coach at Scarborough College, where he was greatly respected by staff and students.

Herbert Sutcliffe

Full name: *Herbert Sutcliffe*

Born: *24 November 1894, Summerbridge, Harrogate*

Died: *22 January 1978, Cross Hills, Yorkshire*

Role: *Right-hand batsman, occasional right-arm medium-pace bowler*

First-class playing career: *1919–1945*

Test record: *Matches 54, Innings 84, Not outs 9, Runs 4,555, Average 60.73, Highest score 194, 100s 16, 50s 23; Catches 23*

First-class record: *Matches 754, Innings 1,098, Not outs 124, Runs 50,670, Average 52.02, Highest score 313, 100s 151, 50s 229; Wickets 14, Average 40.21, Best bowling 3-15; Catches 474*

What happened next: Sutcliffe achieved the best Test average by an England batsman – 60.73, a figure bettered only by Don Bradman (99.94), Graeme Pollock (60.97) and George Headley (60.83). He is one of only seven men to have scored more than 50,000 first-class runs, while no one has beaten his tally of 38,558 runs and 112 first-class centuries for Yorkshire. After retirement, Sutcliffe ran a sports' goods business and held a managerial position with a paper manufacturer. He was a Test selector from 1959 to 1961 and a prominent member of the Yorkshire committee.

Arthur Mitchell

Full name: *Arthur Mitchell*

Born: *13 September 1902, Baildon Green, Yorkshire*

Died: *25 December 1976, Bradford, Yorkshire*

Role: *Right-hand batsman, occasional right-arm slow bowler*

First-class playing career: *1922–1947*

Test record: *Matches 6, Innings 10, Not outs 0, Runs 298, Average 29.80, Highest score 72, 50s 2; Catches 9*

First-class record: *Matches 426, Innings 593, Not outs 72, Runs 19,523, Average 37.47, Highest score 189, 100s 44, 50s 99; Wickets 7, Average 46.71, Best bowling 3-49; Catches 439*

What happened next: Mitchell's best season came in 1933, when he scored 2,300 runs at 58.97 to earn a place on the winter tour to India. In 1935, he was famously summoned from his rose garden to face South Africa at Headingley when Maurice Leyland fell ill on the morning of the match. Mitchell allegedly told Brian Sellers, who'd driven to his house to pick him up, "Oh, all right then, just let me tidy m'sen up a bit." Between 1945 and 1971, Mitchell coached a generation of young Yorkshire cricketers in no-nonsense fashion.

Maurice Leyland

Full name: *Maurice Leyland*

Born: *20 July 1900, New Park, Harrogate*

Died: *1 January 1967, Scotton Banks, Harrogate*

Role: *Left-hand batsman, left-arm spin bowler*

First-class playing career: *1920–1948*

Test record: *Matches 41, Innings 65, Not outs 5, Runs 2,764, Average 46.06, Highest score 187, 100s 9, 50s 10; Wickets 6, Average 97.50, Best bowling 3-91; Catches 13*

First-class record: *Matches 686, Innings 932, Not outs 101, Runs 33,660, Average 40.50, Highest score 263, 100s 80, 50s 156; Wickets 466, Average 29.31, Best bowling 8-63, 5wi 11, 10wm 1; Catches 246*

What happened next: Leyland was England's leading run-scorer in the 1934 Ashes with 478 at 68.28. He hit three centuries during a series in which only Australia's Don Bradman and Bill Ponsford had a better average. In Leyland's last Test, against Australia at The Oval in 1938, he recorded his highest score of 187 – an innings overshadowed by the then world record 364 of Len Hutton, with whom he shared a second-wicket stand of 382. From 1951 to 1963, Leyland coached Yorkshire's youngsters, to whom he was good cop to Arthur Mitchell's bad cop.

Wilf Barber

Full name: *Wilfred Barber*

Born: *18 April 1901, Cleckheaton, Yorkshire*

Died: *10 September 1968, Bradford, Yorkshire*

Role: *Right-hand batsman, occasional right-arm fast-medium bowler*

First-class playing career: *1926–1947*

Test record: *Matches 2, Innings 4, Not outs 0, Runs 83, Average 20.75, Highest score 44; Wickets 1, Average 0.00, Best bowling 1-0; Catches 1*

First-class record: *Matches 373, Innings 526, Not outs 49, Runs 16,402, Average 34.38, Highest score 255, 100s 29, 50s 78; Wickets 16, Average 26.18, Best bowling 2-1; Catches 183*

What happened next: Barber blossomed after his breakthrough 1932 season, becoming one of Yorkshire's most consistent batsmen. His best return came in 1935, when he scored 2,147 runs at 42.09, including a career-best 255 against Surrey at Sheffield. Also that year, Barber made both his two Test appearances in the home series with South Africa, while he was part of a non-Test playing MCC squad that toured Australia and New Zealand that winter. After hanging up his whites, Barber coached cricket at the North Riding Education Authority and Ashville College, Harrogate.

Brian Sellers

Full name: *Arthur Brian Sellers*

Born: *5 March 1907, Keighley, Yorkshire*

Died: *20 February 1981, Eldwick, Bingley, Yorkshire*

Role: *Right-hand batsman, occasional right-arm off-spin bowler*

First-class playing career: *1932–1948*

First-class record: *Matches 344, Innings 455, Not outs 53, Runs 9,270, Average 23.05, Highest score 204, 100s 4, 50s 45; Wickets 9, Average 75.11, Best bowling 2-10; Catches 273*

What happened next: Sellers became one of the greatest county captains of all time, leading Yorkshire to a further six Championships between 1933 and 1946. He was a Test selector after the war and served as Yorkshire's chairman from 1959 to 1972. Sellers oversaw a further seven Championships in his time as administrator, thus presiding over the two most successful periods in Yorkshire's history. However, he blotted his copybook when he became embroiled in the controversial departures of Brian Close and Raymond Illingworth towards the end of his reign.

Arthur Wood

Full name: *Arthur Wood*

Born: *25 August 1898, Fagley, Bradford, Yorkshire*

Died: *1 April 1973, Middleton, Ilkley, Yorkshire*

Role: *Right-hand batsman, wicketkeeper*

First-class playing career: *1927–1948*

Test record: *Matches 4, Innings 5, Not outs 1, Runs 80, Average 20.00, Highest score 53, 50s 1; Catches 10, Stumpings 1*

First-class record: *Matches 420, Innings 500, Not outs 83, Runs 8,842, Average 21.20, Highest score 123*, 100s 1, 50s 43; Wickets 1, Average 33.00, Best bowling 1-33; Catches 631, Stumpings 255*

What happened next: Wood kept wicket in 225 consecutive Yorkshire matches before Brian Sellers heard him boast of his record at Hove in 1935. "If that's the case, Arthur, you deserve a rest," said Sellers, who promptly gave the gloves to Paul Gibb. When Wood walked out to bat against Australia on his Test debut at The Oval in 1938, with the scoreboard showing 770 for six, he famously quipped: "I was always a man for a crisis." After leaving cricket, Wood devoted increasing time to his hobby of building model galleons.

Arthur Rhodes

Full name: *Arthur Cecil Rhodes*

Born: *14 October 1906, Headingley, Leeds*

Died: *21 May 1957, Headingley, Leeds*

Role: *Right-hand batsman, right-arm fast-medium bowler*

First-class playing career: *1932–1934*

First-class record: *Matches 61, Innings 70, Not outs 19, Runs 917, Average 17.98, Highest score 64*, 50s 2; Wickets 107, Average 28.28, Best bowling 6-19, 5wi 5; Catches 45*

What happened next: Having debuted at the start of 1932, Rhodes had left the county game by the end of 1934. He moved into Yorkshire and Lancashire league cricket when the role of Bill Bowes's pace bowling partner went to Frank Smailes. Bowes thought Rhodes the better bowler but said he paid for trying to do two jobs at once. After playing cricket all day, Rhodes would return to his newsagent's/stationer's business in Headingley and stay until midnight, snatching a few hours' sleep before returning to the ground.

Hedley Verity

Full name: *Hedley Verity*

Born: *18 May 1905, Leeds, Yorkshire*

Died: *31 July 1943, Caserta, Italy*

Role: *Right-hand batsman, left-arm spin bowler*

First-class playing career: *1930–1939*

Test record: *Matches 40, Innings 44, Not outs 12, Runs 669, Average 20.90, Highest score 66*, 50s 3; Wickets 144, Average 24.37, Best bowling 8-43; 5wi 5, 10wm 2; Catches 30*

First-class record: *Matches 378, Innings 416, Not outs 106, Runs 5,603, Average 18.07, Highest score 101, 100s 1, 50s 13; Wickets 1,956, Average 14.90, Best bowling 10-10, 5wi 164, 10wm 54; Catches 269*

What happened next: Verity captured at least 150 wickets in each of the remaining seven seasons up to the war, with a best of 216 at 13.18 in 1936. He also claimed over 200 wickets in 1935 and 1937. After joining the Yorkshire-based Green Howards, Verity rose to the rank of captain and was part of the 1st Battalion that took part in the Sicily landings in 1943. He was hit in the chest by shrapnel during a night-time attack at Catania and died 11 days later in a military hospital.

George Macaulay

Full name: *George Gibson Macaulay*

Born: *7 December 1897, Thirsk, Yorkshire*

Died: *13 December 1940, Sullom Voe, Shetland Islands*

Role: *Right-hand batsman, right-arm medium-pace/ off-spin bowler*

First-class playing career: *1920–1935*

Test record: *Matches 8, Innings 10, Not outs 4, Runs 112, Average 18.66, Highest score 76, 50s 1; Wickets 24, Average 27.58, Best bowling 5-64, 5wi 1; Catches 5*

First-class record: *Matches 468, Innings 460, Not outs 125, Runs 6,055, Average 18.07, Highest score 125*, 100s 3, 50s 21; Wickets 1,837, Average 17.65, Best bowling 8-21, 5wi 126, 10wm 31; Catches 373*

What happened next: Macaulay returned to Test cricket in 1933 after a seven-year hiatus, playing two games against West Indies. He retired in 1935 due to rheumatism and an injury to his spinning finger. Macaulay played league cricket before the war and took nine for 10 in the 1938 Lancashire League Worsley Cup final for Todmorden against Ramsbottom, capturing the first two wickets and the last seven. A member of the Royal Field Artillery in the First World War, Macaulay was an RAF pilot officer in the Second World War when he died of pneumonia, aged 43.

Bill Bowes

Full name: *William Eric Bowes*

Born: *25 July 1908, Elland, Yorkshire*

Died: *4 September 1987, Otley, Yorkshire*

Role: *Right-hand batsman, right-arm fast-medium bowler*

First-class playing career: *1928–1947*

Test record: *Matches 15, Innings 11, Not outs 5, Runs 28, Average 4.66, Highest score 10*; Wickets 68, Average 22.33, Best bowling 6-33, 5wi 6; Catches 2*

First-class record: *Matches 372, Innings 326, Not outs 148, Runs 1,531, Average 8.60, Highest score 43*; Wickets 1,639, Average 16.76, Best bowling 9-121, 5wi 116, 10wm 27; Catches 138*

What happened next: Bowes played until 1947 but was unable to operate at more than medium pace due to the effects of his time as a prisoner of war. He continued to serve the game in the capacity of cricket correspondent of first the *Yorkshire Evening News* and then the *Yorkshire Evening Post*, becoming great friends with the *Yorkshire Post's* Jim Kilburn, his inseparable press box companion. Outside cricket, Bowes enjoyed conjuring tricks and was a member of the Magic Circle. He was Yorkshire's last survivor of the 10 for 10 match.

The Nottinghamshire Side

Walter Keeton

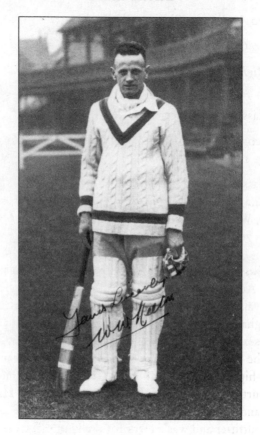

Full name: *William Walter Keeton*

Born: *30 April 1905, Shirebrook, Derbyshire*

Died: *10 October 1980, Forest Town, Nottinghamshire*

Role: *Right-hand batsman, occasional right-arm medium bowler*

First-class playing career: *1926–1952*

Test record: *Matches 2, Innings 4, Not outs 0, Runs 57, Average 14.25, Highest score 25*

First-class record: *Matches 397, Innings 657, Not outs 43, Runs 24,276, Average 39.53, Highest score 312*, 100s 54, 50s 119; Wickets 2, Average 51.50, Best bowling 2-16; Catches 76*

What happened next: Keeton went on to play two Tests, against Australia at Headingley in 1934 and West Indies at The Oval in 1939. Also in 1939, he scored what remains Nottinghamshire's only triple century: 312 not out against Middlesex at The Oval (Eton were playing Harrow at Lord's). When he ended his career, Keeton was Nottinghamshire's second-highest run-scorer behind George Gunn senior (he is now fourth-highest having been overtaken by Joe Hardstaff junior and Tim Robinson). After cricket, Keeton owned a sports outfitter and was a clerk for the National Coal Board.

Frank Shipston

Full name: *Frank William Shipston*

Born: *29 July 1906, Bulwell, Nottinghamshire*

Died: *6 July 2005, Wollaton, Nottingham*

Role: *Right-hand batsman*

First-class playing career: *1925–1933*

First-class record: *Matches 49, Innings 72, Not outs 8, Runs 1,183, Average 18.48, Highest score 118*, 100s 2, 50s 4; Catches 13*

What happened next: Shipston left first-class cricket in 1933 to become a constable in Nottingham City Police Force. He returned to county cricket in 1956, standing for one season as an umpire, before rejoining Nottinghamshire as coach in 1957. Shipston stayed in the role until 1966 and later worked as a newsagent. In 2000, he became the oldest surviving county cricketer and, at the time of his death, aged 98 years and 342 days, he had for some time been the world's oldest first-class cricketer too.

Willis Walker

Full name: *Willis Walker*

Born: *24 November 1892, Gosforth, Newcastle upon Tyne*

Died: *3 December 1991, Keighley, Yorkshire*

Role: *Right-hand batsman, occasional right-arm medium bowler*

First-class playing career: *1913–1937*

First-class record: *Matches 406, Innings 624, Not outs 60, Runs 18,259, Average 32.37, Highest score 165*, 100s 31, 50s 101; Wickets 2, Average 48.50, Best bowling 2-20; Catches 110*

What happened next: Walker lived to an even greater age than Frank Shipston – 99 years and nine days – and shared with him the distinction of having once been the oldest surviving county cricketer. After retirement, Walker continued to manage his sports goods shop in Keighley. The business – later run by his son and grandsons – shut down in 2012 after almost 100 years of operation. Walker's family cited the effect of internet sales, the advent of sports equipment superstores and the general economic downturn as reasons for the closure.

Arthur Carr

Full name: *Arthur William Carr*

Born: *21 May 1893, Mickleham, Surrey*

Died: *7 February 1963, West Witton, Yorkshire*

Role: *Right-hand batsman, occasional right-arm medium bowler*

First-class playing career: *1910–1935*

Test record: *Matches 11, Innings 13, Not outs 1, Runs 237, Average 19.75, Highest score 63, 50s 1; Catches 3*

First-class record: *Matches 468, Innings 709, Not outs 42, Runs 21,051, Average 31.56, Highest score 206, 100s 45, 50s 99; Wickets 31, Average 37.09, Best bowling 3-14; Catches 395, Stumpings 1*

What happened next: Carr was sacked as Nottinghamshire captain in 1934 amid the fallout from Bodyline, which came to a head when he publicly criticised his club for withdrawing Voce from the Australian tour match at Trent Bridge. Carr went to live in Yorkshire and turned to his other main interest – horse racing. For many years, he had horses in training at Middleham, North Yorkshire, and cut himself off from Nottinghamshire cricket, only softening his stance in later life. Carr collapsed and died of a heart attack while shovelling snow at his Yorkshire home.

Arthur Staples

Full name: *Arthur Staples*

Born: *4 February 1899, Newstead Colliery, Nottinghamshire*

Died: *9 September 1965, Redhill, Nottinghamshire*

Role: *Right-hand batsman, right-arm medium bowler*

First-class playing career: *1924–1938*

First-class record: *Matches 358, Innings 512, Not outs 59, Runs 12,762, Average 28.17, Highest score 153*, 100s 12, 50s 70; Wickets 635, Average 29.82, Best bowling 7-20, 5wi 14, 10wm 1; Catches 219*

What happened next: The closest Staples came to playing for England was when he was chosen for the Test trial two weeks after the 10 for 10 game. However, rain ruined the contest at Cardiff Arms Park and only 79 overs were possible. Also in 1932, Staples achieved the bizarre feat of scoring nine runs from a single stroke off Northamptonshire fast bowler Nobby Clark, running five before John Timms conceded four overthrows. Staples retired in 1938 due to sciatica and became landlord of the Shoulder of Mutton pub at Basford, Nottingham.

Charlie Harris

Full name: *Charles Bowmar Harris*

Born: *6 December 1907, Underwood, Nottinghamshire*

Died: *8 August 1954, Nottingham*

Role: *Right-hand batsman, right-arm slow-medium bowler*

First-class playing career: *1928–1951*

First-class record: *Matches 362, Innings 601, Not outs 64, Runs 18,823, Average 35.05, Highest score 239*, 100s 30, 50s 106; Wickets 196, Average 42.82, Best bowling 8-80, 5wi 3; Catches 164*

What happened next: The only Nottinghamshire player in the Headingley match without a first-class hundred, Harris finally achieved his breakthrough innings at the 83rd attempt when he scored 132 against Surrey at Trent Bridge in 1933. Harris played for Yeadon in the Bradford League during the war and returned to Nottinghamshire colours in 1946. Declining health forced his retirement in 1951 and although he joined the umpires' list in 1954, his health deteriorated further and he resigned after only four games. He died of cancer, aged 46.

George Vernon Gunn

Gunn G.V.   C.H.R

Full name: *George Vernon Gunn*

Born: *21 July 1905, West Bridgford, Nottingham*

Died: *15 October 1957, Shelton, Shrewsbury, Shropshire*

Role: *Right-hand batsman, right-arm leg-spin bowler*

First-class playing career: *1928–1950*

First-class record: *Matches 266, Innings 395, Not outs 43, Runs 10,337, Average 29.36, Highest score 184, 100s 11, 50s 56; Wickets 281, Average 35.67, Best bowling 7-44, 5wi 9, 10wm 1; Catches 114*

What happened next: Gunn's career experienced a sharp upward curve from 1935, when he managed 1,000 runs for the first time – a feat he repeated for the next four seasons. He opted to stay in league cricket after the war but did make one last appearance for Nottinghamshire in 1950, recording a two-ball duck against Derbyshire after being recalled in an injury crisis, aged 45. Gunn later coached at Wrekin College, Shropshire, and for Worcestershire from 1953 to 1956. He died at the age of 52 due to injuries sustained in a motorcycle accident.

Ben Lilley

Lilley.

Full name: *Ben Lilley*

Born: *11 February 1894, Kimberley, Nottinghamshire*

Died: *4 August 1950, Forest Fields, Nottinghamshire*

Role: *Right-hand batsman, wicketkeeper*

First-class playing career: *1921–1937*

First-class record: *Matches 373, Innings 513, Not outs 79, Runs 10,496, Average 24.18, Highest score 124, 100s 7, 50s 43; Catches 657, Stumpings 133*

What happened next: The only player Verity did not dismiss at Headingley, Lilley played for another five years and consistently averaged in the upper 20s with the bat. The last of his seven first-class hundreds was also his highest – 124 against Warwickshire at Trent Bridge in 1936. His 779 dismissals for the county have been eclipsed only by Thomas Oates, Bruce French and Chris Read. After leaving cricket, Lilley ran the Forest Tavern in Mansfield Road, Nottingham, before dying at the age of 56 after a long illness.

Harold Larwood

Full name: *Harold Larwood*

Born: *14 November 1904, Nuncargate, Nottinghamshire*

Died: *22 July 1995, Randwick, Sydney, Australia*

Role: *Right-hand batsman, right-arm fast bowler*

First-class playing career: *1924–1938*

Test record: *Matches 21, Innings 28, Not outs 3, Runs 485, Average 19.40, Highest score 98, 50s 2; Wickets 78, Average 28.35, Best bowling 6-32, 5wi 4, 10wm 1; Catches 15*

First-class record: *Matches 361, Innings 438, Not outs 72, Runs 7,290, Average 19.91, Highest score 102*, 100s 3, 50s 25; Wickets 1,427, Average 17.51, Best bowling 9-41, 5wi 98, 10wm 20; Catches 234*

What happened next: Larwood was the leading figure in the Bodyline campaign and the leading wicket-taker too, with 33 at 19.51. However, a broken bone in his left foot sustained during the final Test reduced him to only a handful of appearances in 1933, and he was never again the same fearsome proposition. After retiring, Larwood bought a sweet shop in Blackpool and, in 1950, he emigrated to Australia. A public that once reviled him welcomed him warmly, with members of England touring teams guaranteed a similar reception at his home in Sydney.

Bill Voce

Voce W.   C.H.R.

Full name: *William Voce*

Born: *8 August 1909, Annesley Woodhouse, Nottinghamshire*

Died: *6 June 1984, Lenton, Nottinghamshire*

Role: *Right-hand batsman, left-arm fast-medium bowler*

First-class playing career: *1927–1952*

Test record: *Matches 27, Innings 38, Not outs 15, Runs 308, Average 13.39, Highest score 66, 50s 1; Wickets 98, Average 27.88, Best bowling 7-70, 5wi 3, 10wm 2; Catches 15*

First-class record: *Matches 426, Innings 525, Not outs 130, Runs 7,590, Average 19.21, Highest score 129, 100s 4, 50s 26; Wickets 1,558, Average 23.08, Best bowling 8-30, 5wi 84, 10wm 20; Catches 288*

What happened next: Bodyline also cast a long shadow over Voce's career; he did not represent England again for almost three-and-a-half years. He was England's best bowler on their next tour of Australia, in 1936-37, with 26 wickets at 21.53, and he also toured there in 1946-47. Voce – who finished with more Test wickets and a better Test average than Larwood – coached at Trent Bridge from 1947 to 1952. He later coached at the MCC Indoor School at Lord's, where he was still bowling to schoolboys at the age of 70.

Sam Staples

Full name: *Samuel James Staples*

Born: *18 September 1892, Newstead Colliery, Nottinghamshire*

Died: *4 June 1950, Nottingham*

Role: *Right-hand batsman, right-arm off-spin bowler*

First-class playing career: *1920–1934*

Test record: *Matches 3, Innings 5, Not outs 0, Runs 65, Average 13.00, Highest score 39; Wickets 15, Average 29.00, Best bowling 3-50*

First-class record: *Matches 385, Innings 475, Not outs 95, Runs 6,470, Average 17.02, Highest score 110, 100s 1, 50s 19; Wickets 1,331, Average 22.85, Best bowling 9-141, 5wi 72, 10wm 11; Catches 335*

What happened next: Like his younger brother, Staples retired due to sciatica and, in 1934, he became assistant coach at Nottinghamshire to Jimmy Iremonger. Staples had four years in the role before succeeding Jack Carlin as the club's scorer. Staples, the fourth-highest wicket-taker in Nottinghamshire's history behind "Topsy" Wass, Voce and William Attewell, left Trent Bridge in 1939 to take up a coaching position at Hampshire. He became a first-class umpire in 1949 but was forced to retire after one season due to ill health and died shortly afterwards.

The Umpires

Bill Reeves

Full name: *William Reeves*

Born: *22 June 1875, Cambridge*

Died: *22 March 1944, Hammersmith, London*

First-class umpiring career: *1920–1939*

Tests umpired: *5*

First-class matches umpired: *380*

What happened next: Having officiated three Tests in the mid-1920s, Reeves stood in two more in 1937 and 1939. The last of those, against West Indies at The Oval, was England's final Test match before the war. Reeves had been due to preside over the Fourth Test of the 1938 Ashes at Old Trafford but the game was abandoned without a ball being bowled. He stood in first-class cricket for two decades and was a popular figure with players and crowds, while he had been coaching schoolboys at Lord's just prior to his death, aged 68.

Harry Baldwin

Full name: *Herbert George Baldwin*

Born: *16 March 1893, Hartley Wintney, Hampshire*

Died: *7 March 1969, Hartley Wintney, Hampshire*

First-class umpiring career: *1930–1962*

Tests umpired: *9*

First-class matches umpired: *639*

What happened next: Baldwin stood in nine Tests, the most famous of which was the last one of the 1948 Ashes series at The Oval, when Eric Hollies bowled Don Bradman for a second-ball duck. In 1938, Baldwin caused a stir by no-balling Australian pace man Ernie McCormick 19 times in three overs in the opening tour match at Worcester. McCormick apologised to Baldwin for causing him so much trouble. Baldwin enjoyed a prolific umpiring career that spanned over three decades, while his father, Harry, a former Hampshire player, was also a first-class umpire.

Ten Wickets in an Innings in First-Class Cricket

10-10 Hedley Verity, Yorkshire v Nottinghamshire, Leeds, 1932

10-18 George Geary, Leicestershire v Glamorgan, Pontypridd, 1929

10-20 Premangsu Chatterjee, Bengal v Assam, Jorhat, 1957

10-26 Bert Vogler, Eastern Province v Griqualand West, Johannesburg, 1906

*10-28 Albert Moss, Canterbury v Wellington, Christchurch, 1889

10-28 Bill Howell, Australians v Surrey, The Oval, 1899

10-28 Naeem Akhtar, Rawalpindi B v Peshawar, Peshawar, 1995

10-30 Colin Blythe, Kent v Northamptonshire, Northampton, 1907

10-32 Harry Pickett, Essex v Leicestershire, Leyton, 1895

10-35 Alonzo Drake, Yorkshire v Somerset, Weston-super-Mare, 1914

10-36 Hedley Verity, Yorkshire v Warwickshire, Leeds, 1931

10-36 Tim Wall, South Australia v New South Wales, Sydney, 1933

10-37 Alex Kennedy, Players v Gentlemen, The Oval, 1927

10-37 Clarrie Grimmett, Australians v Yorkshire, Sheffield, 1930

10-38 Samuel Butler, Oxford University v Cambridge University, Lord's, 1871

10-40 Edward Dennett, Gloucestershire v Essex, Bristol, 1906

10-40 Billy Bestwick, Derbyshire v Glamorgan, Cardiff, 1921

10-40 Gubby Allen, Middlesex v Lancashire, Lord's, 1929

10-41 Jack Bannister, Warwickshire v Combined Services, Birmingham, 1959

10-41 Pramodya Wickramasinghe, Sinhalese Sports Club v Kalutara Physical Culture Centre, Colombo, 1991

10-42 Albert Trott, Middlesex v Somerset, Taunton, 1900

10-43 Edward Barratt, Players v Australians, The Oval, 1878

10-43 Tom Rushby, Surrey v Somerset, Taunton, 1921

10-44 Ian Brayshaw, Western Australia v Victoria, Perth, 1967

10-45 Tom Richardson, Surrey v Essex, The Oval, 1894

10-45 Richard Johnson, Middlesex v Derbyshire, Derby, 1994

10-46 William Hickton, Lancashire v Hampshire, Manchester, 1870

10-46 Debasis Mohanty, East Zone v South Zone, Agartala, 2001

10-47 Frank Smailes, Yorkshire v Derbyshire, Sheffield, 1939

10-47 Ottis Gibson, Durham v Hampshire, Chester-le-Street, 2007

10-48 Cyril Bland, Sussex v Kent, Tonbridge, 1899

10-49 W. G. Grace, MCC v Oxford University, The Parks, 1886

10-49 Ted Tyler, Somerset v Surrey, Taunton, 1895

10-49 Eric Hollies, Warwickshire v Nottinghamshire, Birmingham, 1946

10-49 Ian Thomson, Sussex v Warwickshire, Worthing, 1964

10-51 Harry Howell, Warwickshire v Yorkshire, Birmingham, 1923

10-51 Jack Mercer, Glamorgan v Worcestershire, Worcester, 1936

10-53 Bart King, Gentlemen of Philadelphia v Gentlemen of Ireland, Haverford, Pennsylvania, 1909

10-53 "Tich" Freeman, Kent v Essex, Southend, 1930

10-53 Jim Laker, England v Australia, Manchester, 1956

10-54 George Wootton, All England Eleven v Yorkshire, Sheffield, 1865

10-54 Tony Lock, Surrey v Kent, Blackheath, 1956

10-55 Johnny Briggs, Lancashire v Worcestershire, Manchester, 1900

10-58 Shahid Mahmood, Karachi Whites v Khairpur, Karachi, 1969

10-59 George Burton, Middlesex v Surrey, The Oval, 1888

10-59 Stephen Jeffries, Western Province v Orange Free State, Cape Town, 1987

10-61 Peter Allan, Queensland v Victoria, Melbourne, 1966

10-64 Tommy Mitchell, Derbyshire v Leicestershire, Leicester, 1935

10-65 George Collins, Kent v Nottinghamshire, Dover, 1922

10-65 Mario Oliver, Warriors v Eagles, Bloemfontein, 2007

10-66 George Giffen, Australian XI v Combined XI, Sydney, 1884

10-66 Arthur Mailey, Australians v Gloucestershire, Cheltenham, 1921

10-66 Ken Graveney, Gloucestershire v Derbyshire, Chesterfield, 1949

10-66 Ken Smales, Nottinghamshire v Gloucestershire, Stroud, 1956

10-67 Eddie Watts, Surrey v Warwickshire, Birmingham, 1939

10-69 Sammy Woods, Cambridge University v C. I. Thornton's XI, Cambridge, 1890

10-73 Alfred Shaw, MCC v North, Lord's, 1874

10-74 Vyell Walker, England v Surrey, The Oval, 1859

10-74 Anil Kumble, India v Pakistan, Delhi, 1999

10-76 Jack White, Somerset v Worcestershire, Worcester, 1921

10-78 Fergie Gupte, Bombay v Pakistan Combined Services and
    Bahawalpur XI, Bombay, 1954

10-78 Tony Pearson, Cambridge University v Leicestershire,
    Loughborough, 1961

10-78 Pradeep Sunderam, Rajasthan v Vidarbha, Jodhpur, 1985

10-79 Charlie Parker, Gloucestershire v Somerset, Bristol, 1921

10-79 "Tich" Freeman, Kent v Lancashire, Manchester, 1931

10-88 Jim Laker, Surrey v Australians, The Oval, 1956

10-90 Arthur Fielder, Players v Gentlemen, Lord's, 1906

10-90 Jim Sims, East v West, Kingston-upon-Thames, 1948

10-90 Trevor Bailey, Essex v Lancashire, Clacton-on-Sea, 1949

10-92 Imran Adil, Bahawalpur v Faisalabad, Faisalabad, 1989

10-102 Bob Berry, Lancashire v Worcestershire, Blackpool, 1953

10-104 Vyell Walker, Middlesex v Lancashire, Manchester, 1865

10-113 Tom Goddard, Gloucestershire v Worcestershire, Cheltenham,
    1937

10-127 Vallance Jupp, Northamptonshire v Kent, Tunbridge Wells,
    1932

10-129 James Lillywhite junior, South v North, Canterbury, 1872

10-131 "Tich" Freeman, Kent v Lancashire, Maidstone, 1929

10-143 Zulfiqar Babar, Multan v Islamabad, Multan, 2009

10-175 Eddie Hemmings, International XI v West Indies XI, Kingston,
    1982

**10-? Edmund Hinkly, Kent v England, Lord's, 1848

**10-? John Wisden, North v South, Lord's, 1850

In addition, the following instances were achieved in 12-a-side games:

10-36 Fitz Hinds, A. B. St Hill's XII v Trinidad, Port-of-Spain, 1901

10-69 E. M. Grace, Gentlemen of Marylebone Cricket Club v Gentlemen of Kent, Canterbury, 1862

10-92 W. G. Grace, Gentlemen of Marylebone Cricket Club v Kent, Canterbury, 1873

* *On first-class debut*
** *There is no record of the runs conceded by Edmund Hinkly and John Wisden*

(Statistics correct at time of writing).

Bibliography

Ashley-Cooper, F. S., *Nottinghamshire Cricket and Cricketers*, Henry B. Saxton, 1923

Bailey, Philip; Thorn, Philip; Wynne-Thomas, Peter, *Who's Who of Cricketers*, Newnes Books, 1984

Boothroyd, Derrick, *Half a Century of Yorkshire Cricket*, Kennedy Brothers Ltd., 1981

Bowes, Bill, *Express Deliveries*, Stanley Paul, 1949

Cardus, Neville, *Cardus on Cricket*, Sportsman's Book Club, 1949

Cardus, Neville, *Play Resumed with Cardus*, Souvenir Press, 1979

Carr, A. W., *Cricket with the Lid Off*, Hutchinson & Co, 1935

Carr, J. L., *Carr's Dictionary of Extra-Ordinary Cricketers*, The Quince Tree Press, 1977 (new edition, Aurum, 2005)

Chalke, Stephen, *Five Five Five: Holmes and Sutcliffe in 1932*, Fairfield Books, 2007

Davidson, Max, *We'll Get 'Em in Sequins: Manliness, Yorkshire Cricket and the Century that Changed Everything*, John Wisden & Co., 2012

Davis, Sam, *Hedley Verity: Prince with a Piece of Leather*, The Epworth Press, 1952

Douglas, Christopher, *Douglas Jardine: Spartan Cricketer*, Methuen, 2002

Duckworth, Leslie, *Holmes and Sutcliffe: The Run Stealers*, Hutchinson & Co, 1970

Frindall, Bill, (ed.), *The Wisden Book of Test Cricket 1876–77 to 1977–78*, Macdonald & Jane's, 1980

Frith, David, *The Slow Men*, Allen and Unwin, 1984

Frith, David, *Pageant of Cricket*, Macmillan, 1987

Frith, David, *Bodyline Autopsy*, Aurum, 2002

Frith, David, *Frith on Cricket*, Great Northern Books, 2010

Gardiner, Juliet, *The Thirties: An Intimate History*, Harper Press, 2011

Green, Benny, (ed.), *Wisden Anthology 1864–1900*, Queen Anne Press, 1979

Green, Benny, (ed.), *Wisden Anthology 1900–1940*, Queen Anne Press, 1980

Hamilton, Duncan, (ed.), *Sweet Summers: The Classic Cricket Writing of JM Kilburn*, Great Northern Books, 2008

Hamilton, Duncan, *Harold Larwood*, Quercus, 2009

Hamilton, Duncan, (ed.), *Wisden on Yorkshire*, John Wisden & Co., 2011

Haynes, Basil; Lucas, John, *The Trent Bridge Battery: The Story of the Sporting Gunns*, Willow Books, 1985

Hayter, Reg, (ed.), *The Best of The Cricketer 1921–1981*, Cassell, 1981

Hill, Alan, *Hedley Verity: A Portrait of a Cricketer*, Kingswood, 1986 (reissued version, Mainstream, 2000)

Hodgson, Derek, *The Official History of Yorkshire County Cricket Club*, The Crowood Press, 1989

Holloway, David (ed.), *The Thirties: A Chronicle of the Decade*, Simon & Schuster, 1993

Hutton, Len, *Cricket is My Life*, Hutchinson & Co., 1949

Hutton, Len, *Just My Story*, Hutchinson & Co., 1956

Hutton, Len, *Fifty Years in Cricket*, Stanley Paul, 1984

Jennings, Grenville, *Nottinghamshire Cricketers on Old Picture Postcards*, Reflections of a Bygone Age, 1980

Kay, John, (ed.), *Cricket Heroes*, The Cricket Writers' Club, Phoenix Sports Books, 1959

Kilburn, J. M., *In Search of Cricket*, Arthur Barker, 1937

Kilburn, J. M.; Nash, J. H., *History of Yorkshire County Cricket 1924–1949*, Yorkshire County Cricket Club, 1950

Kilburn, J. M., *Yorkshire*, Convoy, 1950

Kilburn, J. M., *A History of Yorkshire Cricket*, Stanley Paul, 1970

Kilburn, J. M., *Thanks to Cricket*, Stanley Paul, 1972

Kilburn, J. M., *Overthrows*, Stanley Paul, 1975

Larwood, Harold; Perkins, Kevin, *The Larwood Story*, Bonpara Pty, 1982

Ledbetter, Jim, *100 Greats: Nottinghamshire County Cricket Club*, Tempus, 2003

Lemmon, David, *Cricket's Champion Counties*, Breedon Books, 1991

Lucy, Nick; Dalling, Harry, *Nottinghamshire County Cricket Club: A Man for 40 Seasons*, Archive Publications, 1988

Marshall, John, *Headingley*, Pelham Books, 1970

Mills, Robert, *Field of Dreams: Headingley 1890–2001*, Great Northern Books, 2001

Nottinghamshire County Cricket Club Yearbook, various editions

Pope, Mick; Dyson, Paul, *100 Greats: Yorkshire County Cricket Club*, Tempus, 2001

Porter, Dilwyn, *Yesterday's Britain*, Reader's Digest, 1998

Pullin, A. W., *History of Yorkshire County Cricket 1903–1923*, Chorley & Pickersgill, 1924

Rickson, Barry, *Hedley Verity: Famous Cricketers Series*, Association of Cricket Statisticians and Historians, 1999

Robertson-Glasgow, R. C., *Cricket Prints: Some Batsmen and Bowlers 1920-1940*, T. Werner Laurie, 1943

Robertson-Glasgow, R. C., *More Cricket Prints: Some Batsmen and Bowlers 1920-1945*, T. Werner Laurie, 1948

Rogers, Byron, *The Last Englishman: The Life of JL Carr*, Aurum, 2002

Rosenwater, Irving, *Sir Donald Bradman: A Biography*, Batsford, 1978

Ross, Gordon, *Cricket's Great Characters*, G. Ross, 1977

Sutcliffe, Herbert, *For England and Yorkshire*, Edward Arnold & Co., 1935

Thacker, Matt, (ed.), *The Nightwatchman, Issue 1 (Verity's War by James Holland)*, John Wisden & Co., 2013

Thomas, Peter, *Yorkshire Cricketers 1839-1939*, Hodgson, 1973

Thomson, A. A., *Hirst and Rhodes*, The Epworth Press, 1959

Verity, Hedley, *Bowling 'Em Out*, Hutchinson & Co., 1936

Warner, David, *The Sweetest Rose: 150 Years of Yorkshire County Cricket Club 1863–2013*, Great Northern Books, 2012

Williams, Marcus, (ed.), *Double Century: 200 Years of Cricket in The Times*, Collins, 1985

Wisden Cricketers' Almanack, various editions

Woodhouse, Anthony, *The History of Yorkshire County Cricket Club*, Christopher Helm, 1989

Wynne-Thomas, Peter, *Nottinghamshire Cricketers 1919–1939*, Nottinghamshire County Cricket Club, 1980

Wynne-Thomas, Peter, *Trent Bridge: A History of the Ground to Commemorate the 150th Anniversary (1838–1988)*, Nottinghamshire County Council in association with Nottinghamshire County Cricket Club, 1987

Wynne-Thomas, Peter, *The History of Nottinghamshire County Cricket Club*, Christopher Helm, 1992

Yorkshire County Cricket Club Yearbook, various editions

Acknowledgements

My thanks to the late Frank Shipston, who unknowingly inspired this book, and the late Douglas Verity, who encouraged me to write it. I was privileged to count Douglas as a friend in the short time I knew him and will treasure his memory always. Thanks also to his widow, Ann, one of the nicest people I have met, and to Frank Shipston's son, Peter, for kindly answering follow-up enquiries. I am also grateful to the late John Robert Richardson and his ever-helpful daughter Rosemary Norkett, as well as her equally helpful husband, Stan.

A special thank you to Sidney Fielden, who supplied me with various research items including a typed-up copy of Hedley Verity senior's memoir. Sidney was Douglas Verity's best friend and he admired Hedley Verity to the extent that Douglas used to joke that Sidney thought more about his father than he did. Likewise, I am greatly obliged to those who cast a sagacious eye over the manuscript: the writers Stephen Chalke and Paul Edwards, the Yorkshire cricket lover Ron Deaton and the Nottinghamshire County Cricket Club librarian Peter Wynne Thomas, all of whom helped beyond the call of duty. Not only did they make any number of insightful suggestions, they also spared me from more errors than might otherwise remain.

For help with pictures, my thanks again to Peter Wynne-Thomas and Ron Deaton especially, plus Duncan Anderson,

Madeleine Deaton, Tony Debenham, David Frith, David Hall, Ted Kirwan, William H. Roberts, Iain Taylor, Jon Wager, Nottinghamshire County Cricket Club, the Verity family and Yorkshire County Cricket Club.

I would also like to thank David Allan, Bob Appleyard, Robert Carr, Duncan Hamilton, the late Mary Kilburn and Roy D. Wilkinson. Apologies to anyone I've forgotten.

This book could not have been written without access to old newspapers and, for that, I am indebted to staff at the *Yorkshire Post*, Leeds Central Library, Nottingham Central Library, *Nottingham Post* and *Halifax Courier*.

Last but not least, my thanks to publisher Charlotte Atyeo and the team at Bloomsbury.